W9-AAL-886

■ DRUGS
The Straight Facts

Nicotine

DRUGS The Straight Facts

Alcohol

Cocaine

Hallucinogens

Heroin

Marijuana

Nicotine

■ DRUGS
The Straight Facts

Nicotine

Heather Lehr Wagner

Consulting Editor
David J. Triggle
University Professor
School of Pharmacy and Pharmaceutical Sciences
State University of New York at Buffalo

CHELSEA HOUSE
PUBLISHERS
A Haights Cross Communications Company
Philadelphia

CHELSEA HOUSE PUBLISHERS
VP, NEW PRODUCT DEVELOPMENT Sally Cheney
DIRECTOR OF PRODUCTION Kim Shinners
CREATIVE MANAGER Takeshi Takahashi
MANUFACTURING MANAGER Diann Grasse

Staff for NICOTINE
ASSOCIATE EDITOR Bill Conn
PRODUCTION EDITOR Jaimie Winkler
PHOTO RESEARCHER Noelle Nardone
SERIES & COVER DESIGNER Terry Mallon
LAYOUT 21st Century Publishing and Communications, Inc.

A Haights Cross Communications ◀ Company

http://www.chelseahouse.com

First Printing

1 3 5 7 9 8 6 4 2

Library of Congress Cataloging-in-Publication Data

Wagner, Heather Lehr.
    Nicotine / by Heather Lehr Wagner.
       v. cm.—(Drugs, the straight facts)
Includes bibliographical references and index.
Contents: Thinking about smoking—The history of tobacco—The health
effects of nicotine and smoking—Teenage trends and attitudes—Nicotine
addiction—Exploring additional resources.
    ISBN 0-7910-7264-9
    1. Tobacco habit—Juvenile literature. 2. Nicotine—Juvenile literature.
[1. Tobacco habit. 2. Nicotine. 3. Smoking.] I. Title. II. Series.
HV5732.W34 2003
362.29'6—dc21

                                                    2002155985

Table of Contents

The Use and Abuse of Drugs

The issues associated with drug use and abuse in contemporary society are vexing subjects, fraught with political agendas and ideals that often obscure essential information that teens need to know to have intelligent discussions about how to best deal with the problems associated with drug use and abuse. *Drugs: The Straight Facts* aims to provide this essential information through straightforward explanations of how an individual drug or group of drugs works in both therapeutic and non-therapeutic conditions; with historical information about the use and abuse of specific drugs; with discussion of drug policies in the United States; and with an ample list of further reading.

From the start, the series uses the word *"drug"* to describe psychoactive substances that are used for medicinal or non-medicinal purposes. Included in this broad category are substances that are legal or illegal. It is worth noting that humans have used many of these substances for hundreds, if not thousands of years. For example, traces of marijuana and cocaine have been found in Egyptian mummies; the use of peyote and Amanita fungi has long been a component of religious ceremonies worldwide; and alcohol production and consumption have been an integral part of many human cultures' social and religious ceremonies. One can speculate about why early human societies chose to use such drugs. Perhaps, anything that could provide relief from the harshness of life—anything that could make the poor conditions and fatigue associated with hard work easier to bear—was considered a welcome tonic. Life was likely to be, according to the seventeenth century English philosopher Thomas Hobbes, *"poor, nasty, brutish and short."* One can also speculate about modern human societies' continued use and abuse of drugs. Whatever the reasons, the consequences of sustained drug use are not insignificant—addiction, overdose, incarceration, and drug wars—and must be dealt with by an informed citizenry.

The problem that faces our society today is how to break

the connection between our demand for drugs and the willingness of largely outside countries to supply this highly profitable trade. This is the same problem we have faced since narcotics and cocaine were outlawed by the Harrison Narcotic Act of 1914, and we have yet to defeat it despite current expenditures of approximately $20 billion per year on "the war on drugs." The first step in meeting any challenge is always an intelligent and informed citizenry. The purpose of this series is to educate our readers so that they can make informed decisions about issues related to drugs and drug abuse.

SUGGESTED ADDITIONAL READING

David T. Courtwright, *Forces of Habit. Drugs and the making of the modern world.* Cambridge, Mass.: Harvard University Press, 2001. David Courtwright is Professor of History at the University of North Florida.

Richard Davenport-Hines, *The Pursuit of Oblivion. A global history of narcotics.* New York: Norton, 2002. The author is a professional historian and a member of the Royal Historical Society.

Aldous Huxley, *Brave New World.* New York: Harper & Row, 1932. Huxley's book, written in 1932, paints a picture of a cloned society devoted to the pursuit only of happiness.

David J. Triggle
University Professor
School of Pharmacy and Pharmaceutical Sciences
State University of New York at Buffalo

1

Thinking About Smoking

Most teens begin smoking for one simple reason: "It makes me look good." They feel that smoking somehow transforms them into someone tougher, or cooler, or older. In movies, we see our favorite actors and actresses smoking, looking more glamorous, more sophisticated while holding a cigarette. Smoking seems like a quick and easy way to change the way you feel about yourself and the way others feel about you.

But smoking is more than just an image, and anyone who has seen a friend or family member struggle with the health problems caused by a lifetime of smoking knows that smokers pay a price for their habit. What we don't see in the movies are the discolored teeth and fingers, the phlegm (mucus)-filled cough, and the rasping voice—all of which reveal the true results of smoking.

Smoking is more than just a habit, more than just "looking good." It is addictive. Cigarette smoking is the leading cause of preventable death. According to the U.S. Centers for Disease Control and Prevention, more than 400,000 people die every year from smoking-related diseases—more than the annual deaths caused by alcohol, AIDS, traffic accidents, drug abuse, murder, and suicide combined. And even more people are affected secondhand, suffering health problems caused by exposure to the smoking of others.

A cigarette is a thin roll of finely chopped tobacco wrapped in paper. It is also what scientists refer to as a drug delivery system: it provides the means to deliver a drug, nicotine, into the body.

WHAT IS NICOTINE?

When we think of drug abuse, we may not think about cigarettes. But cigarettes are addictive because they contain a drug—nicotine. Nicotine is a stimulant, and just like cocaine, amphetamines, or methamphetamines, nicotine works by

Targeting Tobacco Use:
The Nation's Leading Cause of Death
2002

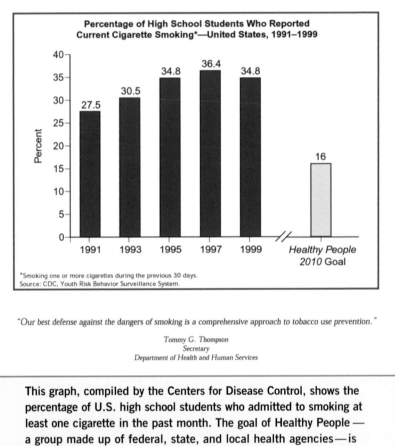

Percentage of High School Students Who Reported Current Cigarette Smoking*—United States, 1991–1999

*Smoking one or more cigarettes during the previous 30 days.
Source: CDC, Youth Risk Behavior Surveillance System.

"Our best defense against the dangers of smoking is a comprehensive approach to tobacco use prevention."

Tommy G. Thompson
Secretary
Department of Health and Human Services

This graph, compiled by the Centers for Disease Control, shows the percentage of U.S. high school students who admitted to smoking at least one cigarette in the past month. The goal of Healthy People — a group made up of federal, state, and local health agencies—is to cut these percentages by more than half by 2010.

speeding up the processing rate of the central nervous system. Nicotine is highly addictive, and smokers can quickly become dependent on cigarettes and suffer serious symptoms of withdrawal when they try to quit.

Nicotine use has a history that dates back to the earliest records of settlers arriving in America. American Indians introduced these settlers to the tobacco plant. Explorers like Christopher Columbus encountered tobacco in the 1400s during their earliest journeys to the New World. Tobacco is a plant that is native to North America and other parts of the Western Hemisphere. And the tobacco plant contains nicotine as its major mood-altering ingredient.

Nicotine is really a poisonous alkaloid (a compound that contains carbon and nitrogen and is found in some plants; some are poisonous, others can be used for medicinal purposes). Nicotine travels through the body, affecting the brain and central nervous system, the hypothalamus, and pituitary gland (meaning that it affects the hormone system), and then accumulates in the brain. It moves fast. When you smoke a cigarette, nicotine races through your body, reaching your brain within 10 seconds from the time you inhale. But its effects also disappear quickly—within only a few minutes—meaning that you need to smoke more and more often to maintain the feelings you get from smoking.

What are these feelings? Nicotine mimics the actions of the hormone epinephrine (also known as adrenaline) and the neu- rotransmitter acetylcholine in the brain. (A neurotransmitter is a substance that sends nerve impulses in the brain.) These feel- ings make you feel more alert. Nicotine also causes the release of endorphins, which make you feel more calm, and dopamine, a substance that enhances your feelings of pleasure. In this way, nicotine functions both as a stimulant and a depressant.

Nicotine is only one of the ingredients in cigarettes. In the United States, tobacco products such as cigarettes are made from a blend of different types of tobacco leaves, and then sugar and other flavorings are added. Most American cigarettes are made from a "lighter" blend of tobacco, which produces an acidic smoke when it is burned. Other tobacco products, such as those used in pipes and cigars, burn a darker tobacco, which gives off an alkaline smoke. Why does this matter? The pH content (acid/alkaline balance) of the smoke determines how much nicotine is absorbed through your mouth when you smoke. In general, the darker and more alkaline the tobacco, the more nicotine is absorbed in your mouth.

Kelly's best friend was the first one to smoke. She had taken a few cigarettes from the pack her aunt kept in her purse. Now, all of Kelly's friends sneak cigarettes, stealing them from adults or borrowing them from each other. They smoke outside, walking around the mall, even in the bathroom in school. Kelly feels left out. The other girls look older and more sophisticated when they smoke. It is as if they are members of some elite group.

The first time Mark tried smoking a cigarette, he thought he was going to be sick. He coughed and coughed, gasping for air while his friends laughed at him. He felt nauseous for a long time afterward. But his friends all smoked, and Mark was determined to fit in. Now, Mark is part of a group that sneaks cigarettes whenever they can. Smoking no longer makes him cough or feel sick to his stomach. It makes him feel relaxed and in control. In fact, he really likes the way he feels when he is smoking. It is when he stops smoking that he doesn't feel so good.

What Kelly and Mark may not know about cigarettes is that they contain nicotine, an addictive drug, in addition to a long list of other toxic chemicals. Like Kelly's friends, many teens start smoking to fit in with their friends. And like Mark, most people cough and feel sick when they smoke their first cigarette. These reactions are the body's natural defense mechanisms working to expel a harmful substance.

To make cigarettes, manufacturers often use tobacco sheet—essentially a kind of reconstituted tobacco. Scraps and stems of the tobacco plant are mixed with other additives, and then added to the blended tobacco leaf.

Recent studies have shown that tobacco manufacturers are able to adjust the nicotine content of cigarettes to control how much nicotine the cigarettes contain. How do they do this? By extracting the nicotine from the tobacco leaf and then adding it back to the tobacco in controlled amounts, manufacturers can ensure a more even distribution of nicotine in each cigarette. Some critics have suggested that manufacturers also do this to ensure that smokers ingest enough nicotine to become addicted. Some of the debates surrounding the manufacture and marketing of cigarettes are discussed later in this book.

IT'S ONLY A CIGARETTE

Within a few seconds from the time you first inhale tobacco smoke, some 4,000 toxic chemicals are being absorbed into your bloodstream, then carried throughout your body. You may be surprised to learn exactly what is in tobacco smoke. Of course, there is nicotine, as well as water. But cigarette smoke also contains tar. It contains carbon monoxide, hydrogen cyanide, nitrogen oxides, ammonia, benzene, formaldehyde, nitrosamines, vinyl chloride, polycyclic hydrocarbons, polonium-210, lead, and arsenic—all toxic.

When you smoke, traces of nicotine can be found throughout your body, even in your hair and eyes. And these toxic chemicals ultimately cause serious and severe health problems. Smoking is the single leading cause of lung cancer, but smoking contributes to many other illnesses. Smoking is a major cause of respiratory illnesses. It causes heart disease and stroke. It can lead to hearing loss and loss of vision. It contributes to bladder cancer, pancreas cancer, kidney cancer, and stomach cancer. Pregnant mothers who smoke are more likely to have babies who suffer from mental and developmental retardation. Smoking also leads to premature aging—your skin becomes wrinkled more quickly.

Teens need to be aware that the most serious risks of addiction to nicotine are associated with young smokers. Basically, the younger you are when you start smoking, the more likely you are to become addicted, the harder it will be for you to quit, and the more cigarettes you will smoke as an adult.

BEYOND CIGARETTES

When we talk about nicotine use in tobacco products in this book, we are speaking principally about cigarettes. Most of the tobacco consumed worldwide—roughly 85 percent—is consumed in cigarettes. But other products contain nicotine, and it is important to remember that these also pose a health hazard because of the nicotine they contain. Cigars, pipes, and forms of smokeless tobacco, such as chewing tobacco (in plug, loose-leaf, or twist form), pan or betel quid, and snuff, should not be viewed as less dangerous or less addictive than cigarettes.

Pipes were one of the earliest forms for consuming tobacco, and their use dates back some 2,000 years. The American Indians smoked tobacco in many of their ceremonies, and they in turn shared their custom with European explorers, who then carried the pipe-smoking habit back to their native countries.

A pipe is constructed from two main connecting parts—a hollow stem and a bowl. Tobacco is placed in the bowl of the pipe and then lit. The smoke from the burning tobacco is pulled into the mouth, traveling up the stem.

Cigars are tightly rolled cylinders of dried tobacco. The most expensive cigars are rolled by hand, but most ordinary, mass-market cigars are rolled by machines. There are three types of cigars: cigarillos—small, slender cigars; pantelas—longer, slim cigars; and coronas—larger, thick cigars. Most cigars have three parts, each containing a different type of

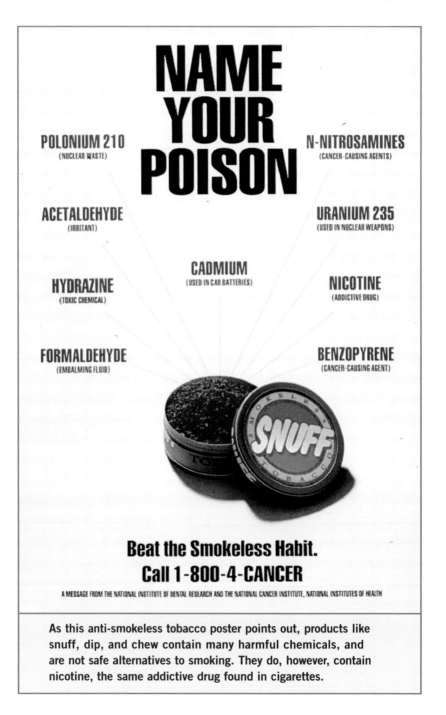

As this anti-smokeless tobacco poster points out, products like snuff, dip, and chew contain many harmful chemicals, and are not safe alternatives to smoking. They do, however, contain nicotine, the same addictive drug found in cigarettes.

tobacco. The inside of the cigar consists of filler tobacco leaves, which are held together by a binder leaf. The binder leaf is then wrapped, surrounded by what is called a wrapper leaf.

Pipes, smokeless tobacco products such as chewing tobacco, and cigars all contain nicotine, and all are hazardous. No single tobacco product is somehow safer or less addictive than another. Chewing tobacco causes lesions to develop in your mouth and causes the gums to decay. Smoking any tobacco product can lead to lung disease. The use of tobacco products in any form increases your risks for developing many diseases.

FAMOUS DEAD SMOKERS

A big part of the decision to start smoking has to do with how the smoker looks: cool, rebellious, tough. Some very famous people have been smokers, many of whom have died due to smoking-related illnesses. See if you recognize any of the famous smokers below, or the diseases that killed them:

SMOKER	CLAIM TO FAME	SMOKING-RELATED ILLNESS
Louis Armstrong	Jazz musician	Heart attack
Lucille Ball	Actress, *I Love Lucy*	Aortic aneurysm
Humphrey Bogart	Actor, *Casablanca*	Cancer of esophagus
John Candy	Actor, *Planes, Trains, and Automobiles*	Heart attack
Walt Disney	Animator, Disney World	Lung cancer
F. Scott Fitzgerald	Writer, *The Great Gatsby*	Heart attack
Ian Fleming	Writer, James Bond novels	Heart attack
Sigmund Freud	Psychologist	Cancer of the jaw
George Harrison	Musician, *The Beatles*	Throat cancer
Bob Marley	Reggae musician	Lung cancer
Jackie Kennedy -Onassis	First Lady	non-Hodgkins Lymphoma
Babe Ruth	Baseball player	Naso-pharyngeal cancer

MAKING WISE CHOICES

Tobacco products are widely available and legally sold in grocery stores, 24-hour convenience markets, gas stations, and many other shops to anyone over the age of 18. But it is important to remember that they contain a drug that is highly addictive—nicotine. Nicotine can affect the way your body works now and how well it may function in the future.

In this book, you will read about teens making decisions about smoking. You will learn more about how nicotine affects the body. You will learn about the legal issues surrounding nicotine and how these laws have changed over the years. You will find out some surprising statistics about nicotine and learn more about the people most likely to smoke or use other nicotine products. Finally, you will learn what to do about nicotine addiction—how to prevent problems, how to ask for help if you want to quit, and what to do if you want to encourage a friend or family member to stop smoking. This information will help you make wise choices when you are dealing with nicotine.

Perhaps you have already tried cigarettes. Maybe you have a friend or family member who is a heavy smoker and whom you would like to help quit smoking. Through the stories of the teens in this book and the facts contained in each chapter, you will learn more about nicotine and begin to understand how it can affect you.

2

The History of Tobacco

The plant known as tobacco played a vital role in the earliest days of the New World, and the development of tobacco as an industry mirrors the civilization and, ultimately, industrialization of much of the Americas. Before a single European explorer set foot on the soil of the famed New World, tobacco was there. The plant flourished across much of the Americas, and tobacco crops could be found from Brazil to the St. Lawrence River.

Native American tribes cultivated tobacco and used it both in ceremonies and for their personal enjoyment. The tobacco plant's leaves were dried and then crumbled. In northern climates, tobacco was chewed or smoked in pipes; for Native Americans in North America, the so-called "peace pipe" was a sacred object. In tropical climates, tobacco leaves were more commonly wrapped together or wrapped around corn husks and smoked as a kind of cigar.

When Christopher Columbus and his crew arrived in the New World in 1492, landing in the territory we know today as the Bahamas, they encountered a native tribe who presented the strangers with gifts: beads, fruit, and some dried leaves. The beads and fruit were appreciated, but the dried leaves were quickly tossed away. Europeans did not yet recognize the value of those dried leaves of tobacco—but they would quickly learn.

Traveling westward, Columbus sailed to the island now called Cuba. Another team of explorers was sent ashore, who returned with reports of the natives inhaling the smoke of a native plant. The

European explorers of the New World were given tobacco leaves as gifts from Native Americans, who smoked tobacco both in religious ceremonies and recreationally. Tobacco use became a worldwide phenomenon soon afterwards.

pipe they used to inhale the smoke was shaped like the letter Y, and the Native Americans called it *toboca* or *tobaga*. Soon the crew was joining the natives in their custom. Smoking was unknown in Europe. Up to this time, smoke was used to cover unpleasant odors or used as incense in religious ceremonies.

Smoking for the sake of inhaling the smoke for pleasure was an unfamiliar concept.

Smoking would not remain an unfamiliar concept for long. Within 125 years, tobacco would spread around the world, carried back by explorers as one of the wonders they discovered in the New World. Tobacco traveled to Spain, Italy, and Portugal. Dutch and Portuguese sailors carried it with them to China, Japan, and the East Indies. Sir Walter Raleigh carried it back to England.

Tobacco spread to France in the mid 1500s, courtesy of the French ambassador to Portugal, a man named Jean Nicot. Nicot was impressed by Portuguese doctors who claimed that the tobacco plant had medicinal purposes, including the power to cure ulcers. He swiftly sent some seeds of the plant back to France, accompanied by his own letters proclaiming the wonder of this new "drug" that would soon bear his name—*nicotine.*

Tobacco soon became widely credited for all sorts of miraculous healing and curative powers, perhaps in part owing to the writings of Nicot and also to the traditions of the Native Americans. The natives had claimed that chewing or smoking tobacco protected them from the many illnesses that struck the European explorers who arrived on their shores. Tobacco was declared to be a useful disinfectant, a cure for the plague (an epidemic of infectious disease), a laxative, and a powerful gargle. It was even suggested that tobacco ashes had use as a teeth whitener! Tobacco smoke was declared to be a helpful mood elevator, as well as a memory improver.

PRIZED CROP OF THE COLONIES

The rapid spread of tobacco and the wildly exaggerated claims of its miraculous healing powers concerned many, among them King James I of England. He criticized the claims of tobacco's medicinal purposes and worried about its impact on his kingdom's health. He eventually wrote down his concerns in an essay published in 1604 under a pseudonym, a popularly circulated pamphlet titled *A Counterblaste to Tobacco*. The king soon took a further step to stop the spread of tobacco. He levied a heavy tax on imports of tobacco, intending to put an end to the smelly habit. But his tax had an unexpected result. Tobacco quickly became one of England's richest sources of income, both from the taxes he imposed and from the wealth pouring in from the English colony of Virginia's tobacco crop.

Initially, Virginia's tobacco crop was considered weaker and more bitter than the superior plants grown in the Spanish colonies of Mexico, Cuba, and the West Indies. Early in the seventeenth century, the Jamestown settlement was determined to convert the tobacco grown by the local Powhatan tribe into something that could challenge the successful Spanish product. One of the settlement's leaders, John Rolfe, earned his place in history by marrying the Powhatan princess Pocahontas, but he also played a critical role in transforming Virginia into one of the New World's wealthiest colonies. Rolfe obtained some tobacco seeds from one of the Spanish colonies (probably Trinidad) and blended them with the Powhatan seeds at Jamestown. The result was a darker, stronger tobacco leaf— one that soon proved to be as popular back in Europe as the Spanish export.

King James and the English rulers who followed quickly recognized that the tobacco crop growing in Virginia could provide almost unlimited wealth. The mission of the Virginia colony soon became narrowed to almost a single purpose: grow as much tobacco as possible. More and more Englishmen were encouraged to set sail for Virginia, to plant their own crops and ship them home. Soon, the American colonies were granted a monopoly on all tobacco shipped to England.

As the habit spread throughout England, the colonies ratcheted up their tobacco production. Tobacco became more than a crop and an export in the colonies—it became an alternate form of money. Workers were paid in tobacco, and goods could be bought with tobacco. Lacking enough workers to help tend the expanding tobacco fields, a new trade soon grew in the colonies—a trade in slaves from Africa.

It is interesting to see how tobacco shaped the history of America in these pre-Revolution days. Particularly in the southern colonies, where the climate was especially favorable to growing tobacco, farmers planted the leaf almost exclusively. Rules were passed dictating that tobacco could be shipped only to Britain, and only on British ships. The colonists were dependent on Britain and its merchants for revenue for their crop, as well as for other goods they needed. Soon their discontent began to spread, as they recognized that they were being forced to sell their crops at favorable prices to British traders, when they might obtain better prices at better terms from other sources.

The differences among settlements in the northern and southern American colonies were also affected by tobacco—differences that would spark a civil war in the nineteenth century. Tobacco plantations and farms required greater stretches of land, and so the settlements in the south were widely spread, with few heavily clustered groups of people. There were fewer large towns. Instead, the large privately-held plantations, generally worked by slaves, resulted in a different mentality beginning to develop—a mentality that divided wealthy landowners from those who worked the soil for them. Democratic ideals were harder to find in a region where a handful of aristocratic landowners decided the fate of many who worked for them.

The goals that would shape the American Revolution were shaped by tobacco, too. Although we remember the democratic ideals and principles, economic concerns were what helped to motivate the colonists of Virginia and elsewhere to fight for freedom. Tobacco growers were tired of the heavy taxes England was imposing, and they worried about the debts many of them had incurred from the exploitation of English merchants. They knew they had a valuable crop; they wanted to be able to market it throughout the world.

Tobacco plants were a major cash crop in colonial America, where farmers, especially in the southern colonies, devoted a majority of their land to its cultivation. King James I passed laws and taxes that made American colonists dependent upon English merchants to make profits from their tobacco, which helped fuel the American Revolution.

A REVOLUTIONARY HABIT

The tobacco plant that played a critical role in the early colonization of America was for use in pipes and, later, inhaled by French aristocrats as snuff. Snuff was a kind of powdered tobacco that was pushed into the nose. Its use quickly spread in popularity until nearly every wealthy gentleman in the first half of the eighteenth century owned an elaborately crafted snuffbox. A ritual or ceremony evolved around the habit of taking snuff, but it was very much a symbol of the wealthiest aristocrats. In

France, snuff's association with the hated aristocrats meant that the habit would come to a swift end in the wake of the French Revolution.

Eventually, the snuff habit faded, but the use of tobacco did not. In the Spanish colonies of the Americas, a new way of smoking tobacco had quickly spread back to Spain and, by the early part of the nineteenth century, to France and then to Russia. The cured tobacco leaf was mixed with the sweepings of rolled cigars and then wrapped in a kind of miniature form with paper. The result was something the Spanish called the *cigarito.*

The cigarito was viewed as a kind of poor man's tobacco, made as it was from the leftovers of pipe tobacco and snuff. It was viewed as weaker than the cigar or pipe. Its popularity remained limited, and it wasn't until British soldiers who had fought in the Crimean War (1854–1856) returned from battle that the habit of smoking cigarettes began to spread throughout England. Theses soldiers had been exposed to cigarette smoking by French and Turkish soldiers. The quicker smoke and greater portability (capability of being carried) of cigarettes was much better suited to wartime than the more time-consuming preparation required by pipes or cigars.

A British tobacco merchant named Philip Morris was quick to capitalize on the new habit. His shop had built a trade on selling Cuban cigars and pipe tobacco from Virginia. But when soldiers returning from the Crimean War began to ask for cigarettes, he quickly recognized the new market and the new opportunity. His shop, located on fashionable Bond Street in London, marketed its cigarettes with the assurance that his cigarettes were made in clean factories using only the finest tobacco and paper, as well as a superior brand of cork tipping designed to keep the cigarette from sticking to the smoker's lips. He called his brands of cigarettes Oxford Blues and Cambridge Blues, later also adding the Oxford Oval brand.

Morris carried out an astute bit of marketing, designed to

link his cigarettes to England's finest universities and target an exclusive, upper-class clientele. The ploy was extraordinarily successful. Suddenly cigarette smoking, which had previously been viewed as a dirty habit for the lower-class masses, was targeting the elite university students—the very group that would go on to assume positions of power in England's political and economic circles.

A DUKE'S TOBACCO

While Philip Morris was cultivating the cigarette market in England, tobacco was playing an important role on the other side of the Atlantic. The habit of smoking cigars spread in the mid-1800s, after the U.S. war with Mexico and the subsequent introduction of the stronger form of tobacco to American smokers. Tobacco actually helped to fund the Civil War; tobacco revenues helped to support the South, and tobacco taxes helped to fund the North's war efforts. But for most of the nineteenth century it was cigar smoking or pipe smoking that most Americans associated with tobacco. New York and Philadelphia manufactured large quantities of cigars, and millions of cigars were imported from Cuba.

As pioneers traveled westward, they took cigars with them. Huge cigars, some up to a foot long, moved across the frontier with settlers in their Conestoga wagons, earning them the label "stogies."

The cigarette remained a novelty in the United States, with its growth limited in part by the manufacturing challenges posed by rolling cigarettes. The industry still depended on hand laborers. Workers who were fast at rolling cigarettes could easily find employment, but even the fastest could manage little more than four cigarettes a minute.

It would take a former Confederate soldier named Washington Duke to propel cigarette smoking to a new level. After the war, Duke had returned to his family's farm in North Carolina and discovered that little of it remained, apart from a few tobacco plants. He shaped the family farm into a modest business supplying pipe tobacco and then took a look around for new opportunities. But others seemed to have cornered the market on the kind of "plug" tobacco used for chewing. Washington Duke's oldest son, James Buchanan Duke, had an idea. In England and in New York, a small number of people were smoking tobacco as cigarettes, and there was less competition for this tiny market. In 1881, a new brand of cigarette was introduced: the Duke of Durham brand.

Then, James Buchanan Duke took the family business one step farther. He had heard of a new machine being patented in Virginia—a machine that could make and roll cigarettes. There was little interest in the machine, called the Bonsack after its inventor, James Bonsack. Most tobacco manufacturers believed that their clientele preferred what they perceived as the higher quality of a hand-rolled cigarette.

Three years after the Duke of Durham cigarette was introduced into the market, James Buchanan Duke had transformed his factory into one using the new Bonsack machines to produce cigarettes. It was a gamble, but one that paid off. The machine sliced cigarettes from a massive tube of wrapped tobacco. It could produce an astounding 200 cigarettes a minute and make as many cigarettes in a day as 40 laborers rolling the cigarettes by hand. And it cost only 20 cents to make a cigarette, compared with the 80 cents it cost to produce a hand-rolled cigarette. The savings in production costs enabled the Duke company (known as W. Duke & Sons) to offer cigarettes at a significantly lower price.

W. Duke & Sons also had another revolutionary impact on the tobacco industry—they were the first American company to professionally market and promote their brands of cigarettes. Included in their packs of cigarettes were collectible items—photos of popular athletes and actors, for instance— and coupons that offered discounts or other rewards for bulk purchases of cigarettes.

Many women worked in cigarette factories like this one in Richmond, Virginia at the end of the 19th century, rolling cigarettes by hand. W. Duke & Sons revolutionized the tobacco industry when they started using the Bonsack, a machine that could do the work of 40 laborers.

By 1890, W. Duke & Sons had grown so profitable that it was able to buy out most American competitors, including the R.J. Reynolds Tobacco Company, and consolidate its empire under the impressive American Tobacco Company name. Some 13 British tobacco companies (not including Philip Morris, which instead formed its own American division), concerned that Duke would next begin to buy up their European market, united to form Imperial Tobacco. The two groups competed for several years, cutting prices and offering bonuses to retailers, until they ultimately united in 1902 to form the British American Tobacco Company.

This alliance would dominate the tobacco industry at the beginning of the twentieth century, but a new climate was growing in America under the leadership of President Theodore Roosevelt. As part of Roosevelt's antitrust campaign, dominating monopolies like Duke's tobacco empire were forced to reexamine their practices. (Antitrust laws protected businesses by placing restraints on large dominating businesses, called monopolies.) By 1911, Duke had been ordered by the U.S. Supreme Court to divest its empire, and divisions such as R.J. Reynolds, Ligett & Myers, and others were separated from the parent company.

BRANDING A CAMEL

Although the Duke family shaped the cigarette business, it was Richard Joshua (R.J.) Reynolds who would create the modern cigarette. Once R.J. Reynolds had been separated from the American Tobacco Company, its founder decided to ensure its continued success by focusing on the cigarette market in a new way. Reynolds did not like the kind of tobacco that was being used in cigarette manufacture, and he was concerned that tobacco smoking might be unhealthy. He decided to create a new mix—one based on a combination of pipe tobacco and a mix of American and Turkish tobacco leaves, with additional flavorings added. The result was a cigarette smoke that was noticeably different from other brands on the market, one that was richer than most American blends and lighter than those from Turkey.

With his new tobacco mix, Reynolds faced a market dominated by roughly 50 brands of cigarettes. Rather than use the tobacco in several different brands, Reynolds decided to do something truly revolutionary—his company would focus its efforts on only one brand of cigarette and push that one brand into market dominance.

Reynolds wanted a name for this brand that suggested something vaguely exotic. Turkish blends were considered to be the market leaders at the time, so Reynolds considered and discarded several different names that vaguely suggested the Middle East—names like Kismet and Nabob—before ultimately settling on the name Camel. His marketing campaign built excitement with advertisements announcing "The Camels are Coming." Within one year, Camels alone held 13 percent of the cigarette market, and by 1918—the year Reynolds died— the company he had founded controlled nearly 40 percent of the American cigarette business.

It was the efforts of Reynolds and Duke that ultimately transformed the cigarette business into the dominant, powerful tobacco industry that we know today.

THE SMOKE OF WAR

Cigarette smoking became a national habit as a result of World War I (the United States entered the war in 1917). Soldiers fighting in western Europe quickly became dependent on cigarettes. In fact, during the war the American general John Pershing sent a cable to the American War Department stating: "You ask me what we need to win this war. I answer tobacco as much as bullets."

In the aftermath of the war, a new market had been added for cigarettes: women. Suddenly, cigarette manufacturers began to target women with their marketing campaigns, and women were gradually seen smoking in public, giving cigarette smoking a new kind of social acceptability.

As the first half of the twentieth century unfolded, cigarette smoking was suddenly a national habit. Glamorous movie actors and actresses smoked in the most popular movies; advertisements featured singers and even doctors praising the "smoothness" of one particular brand of cigarette or another.

Still, a few voices critical of tobacco were beginning to be heard. In 1943, the Federal Trade Commission filed a complaint against the four largest cigarette makers, charging them with falsely claiming in their advertisements that their products were harmless. In 1950, a report was published in the *Journal of the American Medical Association,* indicating that in a study of 600 lung cancer patients, more than 96 percent of them had been smokers.

By 1953, doctors were beginning to suspect that there was

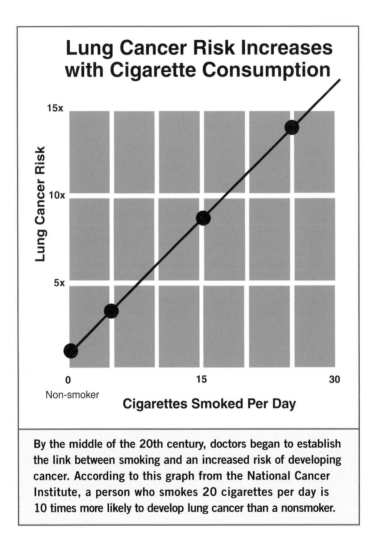

Lung Cancer Risk Increases with Cigarette Consumption

Lung Cancer Risk

15x

10x

5x

0
Non-smoker

15

30

Cigarettes Smoked Per Day

By the middle of the 20th century, doctors began to establish the link between smoking and an increased risk of developing cancer. According to this graph from the National Cancer Institute, a person who smokes 20 cigarettes per day is 10 times more likely to develop lung cancer than a nonsmoker.

an ingredient in cigarette smoke that could produce cancer. Links were beginning to be established between smoking and an increase in the death rate from cancer. There were also new data, published in 1954, which showed that more women were being diagnosed with lung cancer, most of whom had begun to smoke in the 1920s and 1930s.

These studies had an effect on the cigarette market. Sales began to decrease. In 1952, 416 billion cigarettes were consumed;

less than two years later the number had fallen to 388 billion, and surveys showed that 40 percent of the public believed that smoking caused lung cancer.

TOBACCO INDUSTRY RESEARCH COMMITTEE

To combat the public perception that cigarette smoking was dangerous and to avoid a collapse of their businesses, a group of executives from the leading tobacco companies—Philip Morris, American Tobacco, Benson & Hedges, and the U.S. Tobacco Company—held a secret meeting in December 1953 at the Plaza Hotel in New York. They enlisted the services of a public relations firm and agreed to undertake their own campaign, this one attacking the findings of scientists and researchers who were publishing results suggesting a link between cancer and smoking.

This meeting would mark the beginning of what later legal findings would suggest was a conspiracy among executives of the tobacco industry. Their plan was to embark on a public relations campaign that would encourage smokers to continue to smoke, despite key research that was suggesting that smoking posed a significant health hazard. Their decisions centered around four key points:

- To produce brands with filters and brands with lower tar delivery (even though most studies had shown that there was no evidence that any brand of cigarette was less harmful than any other, the idea was to convince consumers that certain brands were "milder")

- To support scientific research that would either deny the earlier research linking cigarettes to cancer or that would, at the least, raise questions about such findings

- To produce a campaign designed to counter the claims of those opposed to smoking

- To diversify tobacco corporations to protect their assets against potential financial losses

New brands appeared on the market—brands with filters and king-sized cigarettes whose advertisements suggested that the longer cigarette length provided "natural filtration." By 1957, nearly 50 percent of all cigarettes sold in the United States were tipped with filters. One of the most popular was Kent, which proudly advertised its "micronite" filter—a filter made from a form of asbestos.

Congress called for hearings on cigarette advertising, and the findings revealed that cigarette advertisements suggesting that cigarettes containing less tar and nicotine were somehow "healthier" were clearly deceptive. By 1959, the Federal Trade Commission (FTC) issued a ruling that tobacco manufacturers could no longer include in their advertisements any statements about low or reduced tar or nicotine. This ruling was designed to eliminate any kind of health claims from cigarette advertising.

NEW WARNINGS

On January 11, 1964, the Surgeon General of the United States, Luther Terry, held a press conference. The 200 journalists in attendance were provided with copies of a 387-page report: *Smoking and Health: Report of the Advisory Committee to the Surgeon General of the Public Health Service.* The report contained the results of a study of thousands of articles and years of research, concluding with the finding that cigarette smoking was clearly a cause of lung cancer in men, was probably a cause of lung cancer in women, and was the leading cause of chronic bronchitis.

At the time that the report was issued, 46 percent of all Americans smoked. More than half of all American men smoked, and one-third of American women smoked. And while the findings of the Surgeon General's report would prompt some people to give up smoking, the number of smokers soon bounced back.

The FTC was quick to act on the Surgeon General's report. Two potential labels were drafted for use on packs of cigarettes.

One read: "CAUTION—CIGARETTE SMOKING IS A HEALTH HAZARD. The Surgeon General's Advisory Committee has found that 'cigarette smoking contributes to mortality from specific diseases and to the overall death rate.'" The other was an abbreviated version: "CAUTION: Cigarette smoking is dangerous to health. It may cause death from cancer and other diseases."

Intensive lobbying by tobacco manufacturers followed the news of these preliminary plans for mandatory labeling. By the time Congress passed the Federal Cigarette Labeling and Advertising Act of 1965, the wording had been changed to the milder "Caution: Cigarette Smoking May Be Hazardous to Your Health."

The question of labeling was raised by Congress again in 1969, and this time a new focus was placed on advertising as well. The sleek cigarette ads were beginning to attract younger and younger smokers, and despite intensive lobbying by the industry, a new law was passed, this one requiring a slightly more strongly worded label: "Warning: The Surgeon General Has Determined That Cigarette Smoking is Dangerous to Your Health." And there was an even more significant ruling as part of this new legislation: as of January 1, 1971, all cigarette advertising would be banned from radio and television.

Another 15 years would pass before Congress would again pass smoking legislation, but the balance was beginning to tilt toward those members of the public supporting an antismoking position. In 1969, Ralph Nader petitioned the Federal Aviation Administration (FAA) to ban the use of cigarettes, cigars, and pipes on all passenger flights, arguing that the smoke posed a health and fire hazard to all on board. By 1974, public sentiment was beginning to build for a modified version of Nader's plan: separate sections on planes for smokers and nonsmokers and a ban on smoking of pipes and cigars.

Only a few weeks after his petition to the FAA, Nader turned to the Interstate Commerce Commission with a

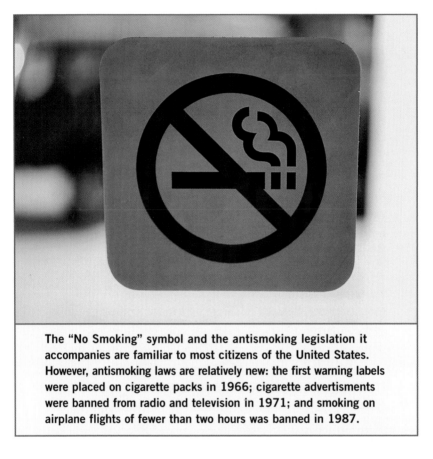

The "No Smoking" symbol and the antismoking legislation it accompanies are familiar to most citizens of the United States. However, antismoking laws are relatively new: the first warning labels were placed on cigarette packs in 1966; cigarette advertisments were banned from radio and television in 1971; and smoking on airplane flights of fewer than two hours was banned in 1987.

complaint about smoking on buses. Within two years, smokers had been confined to the rear 20 percent of interstate buses. Next came interstate rail routes. By 1973, there were separate smoking and nonsmoking rail cars, with approximately half of the train space being designated for smoking cars.

A POWERFUL INDUSTRY

Despite the success of antismoking advocates like Nader, the tobacco industry continued to successfully promote its products. States such as Minnesota, Utah, Nebraska, and Montana all passed laws in the 1970s regulating smoking in confined public places, but no similar federal legislation was passed, in part because no compelling scientific evidence had been published about the effects of secondhand smoke.

In fact, during the first three years after the ban on broadcast advertising went into effect, per capita sales of cigarettes to Americans actually increased. Money that would previously have been spent on broadcast advertising instead went into print media (magazines and newspapers) and outdoor advertising, as well as into increased merchandising and sponsorship of sporting events.

By 1978, a member of President Jimmy Carter's cabinet— Joseph Califano, the Secretary of Health, Education and Welfare—took a bold stand. On January 11, 1978, he announced

K eith last saw his grandfather at Thanksgiving dinner. His grandfather had been battling cancer for several months, and when the family gathered for the holiday meal, Keith was shocked at how thin and frail he had become. The older man didn't say much, and he ate very little. He seemed like a shadow. Keith's grandfather had been a heavy smoker, and his mother said that it was the smoking that had caused the cancer. Later that weekend when he and some friends met at the mall, Keith thought about how sick his grandfather had looked. As they lit up their cigarettes, Keith decided that he would stop smoking before he became too old. He didn't want to end up like his grandfather.

What Keith may not know is that warning labels on cigarette packs have only been around since 1966. The same information about the harmful effects of smoking that is readily available to Keith may not have been available to people in his grandfather's generation. Keith may also not realize how addictive nicotine can be—it may be much more difficult than he thinks to stop smoking.

the start of a major antismoking campaign, one that labeled cigarettes "Public Health Enemy No. 1." He called on schools to teach students about the health hazards of smoking; he called on the Civil Aeronautics Board to ban smoking on all commercial flights; he called on Congress to increase the federal excise tax on cigarettes; and he announced that smoking would be prohibited in his own agency except in specially designated areas. Moreover, he called on other federal offices to do the same.

The FTC next stepped up its own investigation of cigarette advertising, particularly focusing on the targeting of younger smokers. Documents obtained from the tobacco company Brown & Williamson contained the revelation that the company was actively targeting underage smokers by attempting to subtly link cigarettes to marijuana, beer, wine, and sex.

In 1979, Secretary Califano oversaw the release of a new Surgeon General's report, this one reinforcing the health hazards of smoking. The data showed that while the number of smokers had declined, the number of young people smoking had not, and that the number of women dying from lung cancer was steadily increasing. President Carter did little to support the findings of Secretary Califano. Ultimately, Califano was forced out of office.

In 1981, the FTC released the results of a new study showing that the warning label on cigarette packs was having little effect. Congress was ultimately persuaded to act, and the Comprehensive Smoking Education Act of 1984 was passed, requiring rotating warnings on cigarette packs — different messages that would periodically be replaced to inform the public more fully. The warnings stated that cigarette smoke contained carbon monoxide; that "Smoking by Pregnant Women May Result in Fetal Injury, Premature Birth and Low Birth Weight"; that "Smoking Causes Lung Cancer, Heart Disease, Emphysema and May Complicate Pregnancy"; and that "Quitting Smoking Now Greatly Reduces Serious Risks to Your Health."

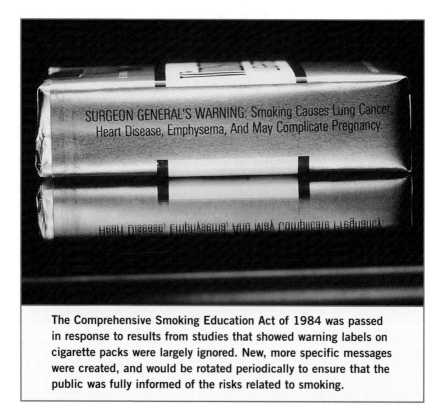

SURGEON GENERAL'S WARNING: Smoking Causes Lung Cancer, Heart Disease, Emphysema, And May Complicate Pregnancy.

The Comprehensive Smoking Education Act of 1984 was passed in response to results from studies that showed warning labels on cigarette packs were largely ignored. New, more specific messages were created, and would be rotated periodically to ensure that the public was fully informed of the risks related to smoking.

In the 1980s, new research was published, much of it supporting the claims that spouses of heavy smokers had a significantly elevated risk of contracting lung cancer than spouses of nonsmokers. A new Surgeon General—C. Everet Koop—issued a report in 1986 that outlined the health consequences of what was termed "involuntary smoking."

The next step came with the decision in late 1981 to form the Coalition on Smoking or Health—a Washington-based group funded by the nonprofit groups the American Cancer Society, the American Lung Association, and the American Heart Association—to move away from merely educating the public on the health hazards of smoking toward a more active approach of lobbying for antismoking legislation. The Coalition's aims were clear, including plans to implement the FTC proposal for larger warning labels with rotating messages on cigarettes and in advertising and to raise the federal excise tax on cigarettes (the tax had remained at 8 cents per pack for nearly 30 years).

The increased federal tax went into effect in 1983, but tobacco manufacturers were prepared. Loudly denouncing the planned tax increase as discriminating against the poor, the manufacturers quietly began to increase prices in August 1982, raising prices four times over a six-month period. When sales of cigarettes dropped approximately 4 percent in 1983, tobacco manufacturers were quick to blame the federal tax. But they were in fact enjoying high profits, thanks to their price increases (the price of a pack of cigarettes rose from 62 cents in 1980 to 96 cents four years later).

In 1984, legislation passed requiring tobacco manufacturers to provide the Office on Smoking and Health with a complete list of the additives they used in manufacturing cigarettes. The results were to be kept secret, to be used only by government researchers to determine whether or not the additives posed a danger. For 10 years, those ingredients would be quietly studied and the results kept locked away. And then, in 1994, under the administration of President Bill Clinton, the Food and Drug Administration (FDA) issued a report stating what researchers had known for some time: cigarette manufacturers appeared to be manipulating the nicotine level in their cigarettes, using additives to keep smokers addicted.

In the late 1980s, antismoking campaigns began to spread throughout the United States. States were soon restricting smoking on public transportation, in elevators, in schools, and in public office buildings.

LAWSUITS AGAINST TOBACCO COMPANIES

Tobacco companies found themselves being sued beginning in the 1950s, as research reporting the hazards of smoking began to be published. Most were single lawsuits, brought on behalf of a single client by a single lawyer. The tobacco industry was able to drag out the legal process and in nearly every instance outspend any other clients, forcing the lawsuits to be dropped in the face of outrageously expensive legal costs.

In the 1980s, the perception of smoking was quite different than it had been in the past decades. Laws had been passed restricting tobacco advertising on broadcast media, warning labels had been added, and some states and offices were restricting smoking. It was in this climate, in August of 1983, that a woman named Rose Cipollone filed a suit against the Ligett Group, Philip Morris, and Loews (the owner of Lorillard), claiming that the tobacco companies had failed to adequately warn her of the risks associated with smoking cigarettes and their addictiveness. Mrs. Cipollone died little more than a year later, and the suit was continued by her husband on her behalf. Ligett was held liable for negligence because it had failed to warn smokers of potential health hazards before 1966 (when warning labels were required on cigarette packs) and because its ads were misleading. The charges against Philip Morris and Loews were dismissed because Mrs. Cipollone had begun smoking their brands after 1966. The ruling required Ligett to pay Mr. Cipollone $400,000 but was overturned on appeal. The law firm representing the Cipollones, having spent some $5 million on the case, was ultimately forced to give up.

In October 1991, another case was brought, this one on behalf of Norma Broin, a flight attendant for American Airlines, and thousands of other nonsmoking flight attendants. The $5 billion class-action lawsuit charged that Brown & Williamson, Philip Morris, R.J. Reynolds, and Lorillard were guilty of fraud for withholding information about environmental tobacco smoke, resulting in many flight attendants contracting heart and lung diseases from their exposure to smoke in plane cabins. (A class-action lawsuit is brought by one or more plaintiffs on behalf of all people in the same

TOBACCO: A TIMELINE

1492   Christopher Columbus first encounters tobacco during his voyage to the New World.

1561   French ambassador Jean Nicot sends tobacco seeds to the French court.

1565   Sir Walter Raleigh persuades Queen Elizabeth I to try a pipe of tobacco.

1604   King James I of England writes *A Counterblaste to Tobacco*, criticizing claims of tobacco's medicinal uses.

1612   John Rolfe produces first successful commercial tobacco crop in Jamestown.

1619   Tobacco becomes the Virginia colony's chief export.

1665   In England, smoking is used as a protection against the Plague.

1776   American Revolution is partially financed by the use of tobacco as collateral for loans.

1856   Soldiers returning from Crimean War introduce cigarettes in England.

1890   American Tobacco Company created by J.B. Duke.

1911   Duke forced to dismantle cigarette empire.

1913   R.J. Reynolds creates modern blended cigarette.

1917   Rations to World War I soldiers include cigarettes.

1964   First U.S. Surgeon General's report on smoking.

1966   First labels containing warnings placed on cigarette packs.

1971   Cigarette advertising banned from U.S. radio and television.

1973   Arizona passes first state law restricting smoking in public places.

1987   Congress bans smoking on flights of less than two hours.

1994   FDA announces plans to regulate nicotine as a drug.

1998   Tobacco industry reaches settlement worth $246 billion.

2000   Supreme Court rules FDA does not have authority to regulate tobacco.

predicament.) The tobacco companies ultimately agreed to a $349 million settlement.

In 1995, another class-action lawsuit was filed, this one was *Castano et al. v. the American Tobacco Co. et al.* The suit charged the tobacco industry with deceiving the public about nicotine's addictiveness. The Ligett Group agreed in March 1996 to a settlement, but the suit ended only two months later, when a federal appeals panel dismissed the case, agreeing that the potential number of plaintiffs (persons bringing suit, thought to be more than 90 million current and future smokers) to the suit made it impossible to manage.

In 1995, yet another tobacco case, *Carter v. Brown & Williamson Tobacco Corp.*, used the company's own internal documents to clearly demonstrate that Brown & Williamson executives knew about the addictiveness of nicotine. The case was settled in favor of the plaintiff, Grady Carter, awarding him $750,000 in damages, with the jury determining that Brown & Williamson was negligent for not warning the public of the danger of their product. The ruling was over-turned on appeal in 1997, but once more reinstated by the Florida Supreme Court in November 2000.

In May 1994, the first tobacco lawsuit was filed by a state rather than an individual smoker. Mississippi's attorney general claimed that his state had suffered financial harm by being forced to provide the financial resources to treat ill smokers. Only a few months later, the attorney general of Minnesota followed Mississippi's example, this time adding the Minnesota Blue Cross/Blue Shield as a joint plaintiff. West Virginia and Florida swiftly followed, and the tobacco companies eventually settled all four cases.

But the precedent had been set. By the end of 1996, 18 other states had filed similar suits, and negotiations had begun to unite all the state suits into a single settlement with the tobacco industry. The Master Settlement Agreement

(MSA) was presented to the public in June 1997, by which time a total of 41 states were included. The MSA, because it was to be a binding decision on behalf of all states and government agencies against the tobacco industry, required congressional action. The bill was introduced in November 1997 and supported by President Clinton. However, the tobacco industry responded with an intensive and expensive ad campaign and a similarly intensive and expensive campaign lobbying Congress. The bill was defeated in June 1998.

That same month, tobacco companies resumed negotiations designed to settle all pending state cases. A settlement was reached in November 1998. Its requirements include:

- Prohibition against targeting youth

- Banning the use of cartoon characters in tobacco marketing

- Making industry records and research accessible

- Restricting sponsorship by brand names

- Banning outdoor advertising

- Banning the prominent placement of tobacco products in stores

- Banning the sale of merchandise bearing tobacco brand names

- Setting the minimum pack size at 20 cigarettes

- Requiring corporate commitment to restrict youth access to cigarettes

In July 2000, another historic case was finally settled. Filed six years earlier, *Howard A. Engle, M.D., et al. v. R.J. Reynolds Tobacco et al.* was the first class-action suit against the tobacco industry to go to trial, the longest civil action in the history of tobacco litigation. It could result in the largest punitive-damages award in U.S. history. The plaintiffs, a group of Florida residents and their survivors who had suffered or died from medical problems caused by their addiction to cigarettes containing nicotine, were ultimately awarded $145 billion in damages.

3

The Health Effects of Nicotine and Smoking

A cigarette is more than a thin roll of finely chopped tobacco wrapped tightly in paper. It is what scientists call a *drug delivery system*. The cigarette provides a way to deliver a drug—nicotine—into your body.

Nicotine is a highly toxic alkaloid—an organic compound containing nitrogen. Morphine and quinine are also alkaloids. Nicotine is actually a colorless liquid. It doesn't turn brown until it is burned.

The ingredients in tobacco products are varied and, in some cases, frightening. Substances such as ammonia, carbon monoxide, formaldehyde (yes, the same substance used to preserve dead bodies), and even arsenic all can be found in tobacco products, and all of them are potentially toxic. But it is nicotine that works primarily on the brain and nicotine that makes cigarettes and other tobacco products so addictive.

When you smoke a cigarette, you deliver a quick jolt of nicotine to your brain. You are absorbing nicotine through your skin and the mucous lining of your mouth and nose, as well as through the lining of your lungs when you inhale. Smoking provides a rapid way of getting this drug into your body; in about 10 seconds, nicotine reaches peak levels in your brain and bloodstream.

WHAT HAPPENS WHEN YOU SMOKE

With that first cigarette, you are not simply delivering nicotine to your brain—you are actually *changing* your brain. How?

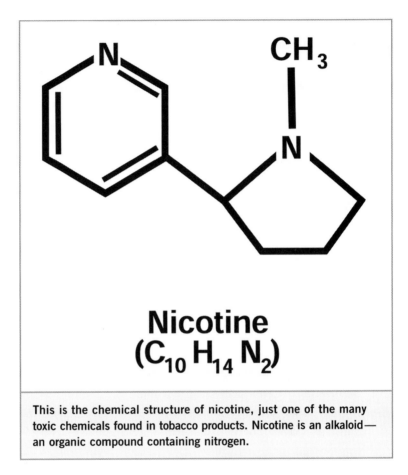

Nicotine
$(C_{10}H_{14}N_2)$

This is the chemical structure of nicotine, just one of the many toxic chemicals found in tobacco products. Nicotine is an alkaloid—an organic compound containing nitrogen.

Nicotine hitches a ride into your body by first attaching itself to the tiny droplets in the burning tobacco. Because they are so small, these droplets can easily pass into every corner of your lungs. Blood that enters the lungs to pick up oxygen also picks up something else—the nicotine. It then travels to your heart, which efficiently pumps it out to the rest of your body.

The nicotine quickly goes to work in your body. Your blood pressure increases by 5 to 10 points. Your heart rate increases by as much as 10 to 20 beats per minute. But it is in the brain that nicotine is quickly transformed from a source of pleasure to a craving or need. Your brain is constantly sending information and signals to your body, often without you even realizing it. For example, when you use the remote control to change the channels on the television, the signal for your finger to click the right button travels from your brain through your brain stem, down your spinal cord, and then through your hand to your finger. You are not aware that these signals are happening, but it involves a complex series of nerve impulses, traveling first as electrical signals, then as chemical signals, and finally back as electrical signals.

These signals, or nerve messages, are carried on part of their journey by substances called neurotransmitters. There are dozens of these neurotransmitters in your nervous system, each specifically developed to carry signals to certain cells called receptors. If you introduce large amounts of certain substances into your body—for example, nicotine—the number of receptors designed to handle this substance increases. This is one of the reasons why nicotine can be so addictive; your nervous system has literally changed to accommodate the drug and will struggle without it.

Let's take another look at the neurotransmitters, the substances in your brain that transmit nerve impulses. There is one type of neurotransmitter, called acetylcholine (or ACh), which plays a critical role in your body's functioning. It plays a key role in the nervous system's regulation of involuntary body processes—actions like regulating your heart rate—and it helps carry messages from one part of the brain to another. Nicotine can copy ACh; any receptors that are geared to respond to ACh respond to nicotine as well. In this way, nicotine can spark the release of other neurotransmitters— neurotransmitters that are normally released in response to the presence of ACh. Nicotine can also prompt your adrenal glands to release adrenaline. It can prompt your blood vessels to release norepinephrine (another neurotransmitter), causing your blood pressure to increase.

THE PLEASURE PRINCIPLE

Perhaps most significant is the way nicotine acts on the part of your brain that regulates feelings of pleasure. ACh releases the neurotransmitter dopamine, a key substance in understanding the addictiveness of many drugs of abuse. Dopamine is normally released by your brain when you are doing something you enjoy—playing with a pet, eating a delicious dessert, spending time with someone you care about, or walking on a beach. When nicotine enters your brain, it triggers the release of dopamine, just as if you were doing one of the things that gives you pleasure. So what's so bad about feeling good?

As we read earlier, when you introduce large amounts of a substance (like nicotine) into your body, the receptors designed to handle that substance change. With nicotine, more dopamine rushes through your system, and the number of receptors—as well as their sensitivity—changes to accommodate this additional dopamine. This means that you will need more and more nicotine, and more and more dopamine, to mimic the pleasure effects of those earliest cigarettes. And in the same way that your brain will interpret the presence of nicotine as one of the most pleasurable experiences you can have, it will interpret the absence of nicotine as one of the worst. It will no longer understand that the lack of nicotine is a "normal" state; it will interpret the lack of nicotine to be a kind of punishment, sparking feelings of anxiety, depression, and irritability.

This is where the cigarette's quick and efficient delivery of nicotine can cause real problems. When you smoke a cigarette, the nicotine in your body reaches its peak level in about 10 seconds. The strongest effects of the nicotine begin to disappear in only a few minutes. Your brain quickly tells you that it needs more nicotine to feel okay. And quickly, an occasional cigarette can turn into a one- or two-pack-a-day habit.

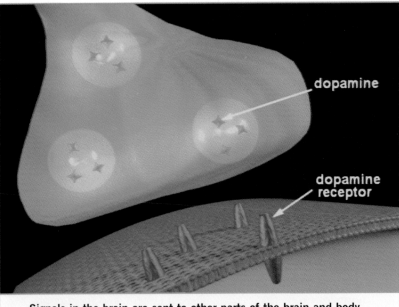

Signals in the brain are sent to other parts of the brain and body through neurotransmitters, or chemical messengers, and neurons, which send and receive these chemical messengers. This is a close-up view of a neuron, and a neurotransmitter called dopamine. Dopamine creates feelings of pleasure when it is released. Under normal conditions, another neurotransmitter called acetylcholine causes the release of dopamine. However, nicotine can mimic acetylcholine, which means that any receptor in the brain that responds to acetylcholine will also respond to nicotine. Therefore, by mimicking acetylcholine, nicotine also releases dopamine and causes the smoker to feel pleasure—a key feature of nicotine's addictive qualities.

THE FIRST WARNING

Your body does not simply passively accept a brand-new substance without a protest. The first time you smoke a cigarette, your body gives a very clear signal that you are inhaling something alien to it. Usually, first-time smokers cough and choke. Some feel nauseous or dizzy, whereas others develop an upset stomach or a headache.

It's surprising that so many people move beyond this

initial experience and continue to smoke. But those who do soon grow accustomed to the presence of nicotine in their body. This is described as developing a tolerance to the drug.

When you develop a tolerance to nicotine, or to any other drug, it no longer produces the same effects on your body as it did at the beginning. Your body has literally grown accustomed to having a certain amount of nicotine in it. You need to take more and more of it to replicate those earlier experiences. This applies to both the pleasant and unpleasant side effects. You will no longer feel ill after one or two cigarettes. You may only feel nauseous or dizzy if you smoke several cigarettes in a row. You also will not feel the same immediate sensation of relaxation or alertness—the stimulation of feelings of pleasure— with only one cigarette. You will need to smoke more cigarettes more often.

Once you become tolerant to a certain level of nicotine, your body experiences withdrawal when you stop smoking. The symptoms of withdrawal include the unpleasant side effects mentioned earlier—things such as irritability, frustration, anxiety, and depression. These symptoms are your body's way of letting you know that it feels the absence of nicotine and that you are physically addicted to this drug.

Nicotine poses the double threat of being both physically and psychologically addictive. Regular smokers become accustomed to feeling a certain level of calm and well-being—the level provided by nicotine. Without it, you will feel more anxious and unsettled—until you have another cigarette.

A HABIT AND A ROUTINE

Although nicotine is the drug contained in tobacco—the drug that proves addictive—we don't often talk about someone being "addicted to nicotine." It's more common to speak of someone needing to "quit smoking" or "break the cigarette habit." This can serve to downplay how addictive nicotine can be; nevertheless, there is a routine that can develop around smoking that can contribute to the psychological dependence people develop on nicotine and make it more difficult to stop abusing it.

Smokers may build a routine around walking or driving a certain route to stop and pick up cigarettes each day. They may smoke whenever they're with a particular group of friends, or whenever they're alone. They may smoke when they talk on the phone, watch television, or first wake up. They may smoke to help deal with negative feelings like stress, anxiety, loneliness, or depression.

When nicotine becomes a part of your routine in this way, linked to feeling better at stressful moments or linked to having a good time with friends, or somehow connected with a regular part of your day, it can be even more difficult to stop using it. In a later chapter, we discuss some methods that may help you or someone you care about to begin to overcome the nicotine habit.

SPECIAL HEALTH CONCERNS FOR TEENS

Nicotine and tobacco use causes many health problems in adults, but the consequences of smoking and using other tobacco products are particularly dangerous for young people. Cigarette smoking during childhood and adolescence can cause severe respiratory illnesses, can decrease your overall physical fitness, and slow down the growth of your lungs and their ability to function. It can leave you gasping for air, increasing how often you cough and how much phlegm you produce.

Take a look at someone who has been a heavy smoker for most of his or her life. You won't be able to see the way the inside of the body has been affected, but the outside offers plenty of clues—rasping voice; stained fingertips, skin, and teeth; and extra wrinkles, particularly around the mouth. Not a pretty picture, is it?

Perhaps you think that this happens only to heavy smokers, and you don't intend to become addicted. You're only

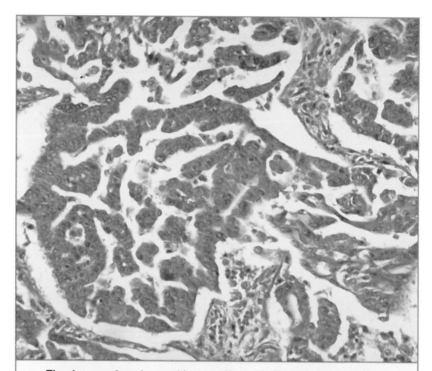

The damage done by smoking manifests itself most clearly in the lungs. This is a magnified view of a stained section of a bronchogenic carcinoma—lung cancer. According to the American Cancer Society, over 80% of lung cancer cases occur in smokers, and only 15% of people diagnosed with lung cancer will live longer than 5 years.

smoking now to fit in or look cool. Maybe you intend to quit when you get older. But research has shown that of all the addictive behaviors, cigarette smoking is the one most likely to start in adolescence—right now, while you're still a teenager. The younger you are when you start to smoke, the more likely you are to become severely addicted to nicotine.

THE DAMAGE
When you follow the path of nicotine through the body of a heavy smoker, you can see how the damage spreads. It begins as cigarette smoke is inhaled into your respiratory system. This is

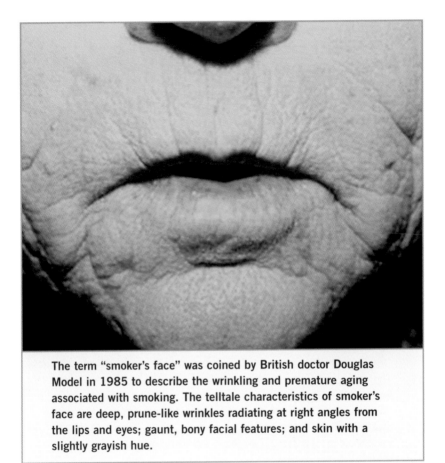

The term "smoker's face" was coined by British doctor Douglas Model in 1985 to describe the wrinkling and premature aging associated with smoking. The telltale characteristics of smoker's face are deep, prune-like wrinkles radiating at right angles from the lips and eyes; gaunt, bony facial features; and skin with a slightly grayish hue.

the part of your body that most clearly demonstrates the damage done by years of smoking. Smoking changes the functioning of your lungs, weakening your defenses against other things you might inhale—things like infectious organisms, particles, or gases. It changes the number and types of cells present in your lungs.

Studies of young smokers have demonstrated this damage to lung structure, especially in the small airways. The longer you smoke, the more likely you are to bring about obstruction of airflow in your lungs.

Smoking next travels on to damage other parts of your

respiratory system. For children and teens who smoke, respiratory illnesses are common. Respiratory problems such as coughing, increased phlegm, wheezing, and shortness of breath all occur.

"SMOKER'S FACE"
How smoking creates wrinkles

A British doctor named Douglas Model coined the term "smoker's face" in 1985 to describe the wrinkling and premature aging associated with smoking. In fact, the smoker's face phenomenon was so common and distinct that Model was able to identify more than half of the smokers with a 10-year-old habit that he saw in his clinic simply by looking at their faces. The telltale characteristics of smoking that he observed were prune-like facial wrinkles radiating at right angles from the smokers' lips and eyes; gaunt, bony facial features; and a slightly pigmented, gray appearance to the skin.

Skin is a dynamic and ever-changing organ that must be renewed continually by the body to stay healthy and youthful. Smoking interferes with the body's ability to break down old skin and replace it with new skin, which leads to the gray, wrinkled skin associated with smoker's face.

Old skin is broken down by special enzymes called matrix-metalloproteinases, or MMPs, that destroy the fibers that form collagen—the connective tissue that makes up about 80 percent of normal skin. The action of MMPs is balanced by MMP inhibitors, which prevent MMPs from breaking down old skin so that skin cells can synthesize collagen to create new skin. Researchers have discovered, however, that smoking disrupts this process and leads to an imbalance between MMPs, MMP inhibitors, and new collagen.

Akimichi Morita and his colleagues at Nagoya City University Medical School performed an experiment that demonstrates how smoking upsets the delicate balance of the skin-renewal

"SMOKER'S FACE"
How smoking creates wrinkles (continued)

process and leads to smoker's face. These researchers exposed human skin cells that produce collagen to a solution of saline (salt water) and cigarette smoke, which mimics the conditions a smoker's skin is exposed to. After one day of exposure to this smoke solution, Morita and his team tested the skin cells and found they had produced high levels of MMPs but not MMP inhibitors. This increased level of MMPs without a comparable increase in their inhibitors caused an increased level of collagen degradation; the skin cells in this experiment produced 40 percent less new collagen than healthy skin cells.

The rapid breakdown of collagen and lack of new collagen to replace it, which is essential to maintaining healthy and youthful skin, is most likely what causes the wrinkles and premature aging associated with smoker's face.

Cigarette smoking also causes heart disease and stroke in adults. Although these diseases are less common in younger smokers, studies have shown that young smokers begin the process, with many developing early signs of cardiovascular disease as young adults. Some studies have also indicated that young smokers develop increased levels of cholesterol, leading to a greater risk for developing heart disease.

SMOKING AND SPORTS

If you are an athlete or enjoy any sport, you need to be aware that smoking affects both your performance and your endurance. When you smoke a cigarette, you reduce the oxygen carrying capacity of your blood. You are also increasing your heart rate and basal metabolic rate—in a sense, working against the very benefits of exercise. Studies of teenage runners show that those who smoked were unable to match the times and distances of nonsmokers.

For the smoker, this is one time that your heart doesn't lie. The hearts of young smokers are slightly different from those of nonsmokers. On standard treadmill tests, smokers cannot perform as well. Their left ventricular mass is increased. Their resting heart rates are two to three beats per minute faster than those of nonsmokers.

Perhaps you have seen a baseball player chewing tobacco, and you thought that this was somehow safer or better than smoking. Think again. So-called "smokeless tobacco," particularly when used by teens, leads to periodontal degeneration (the decaying of your gums). It causes you to develop lesions in

Tim wanted to stop smoking. His track coach had told him that his times were disappointing this season—he wasn't running as fast as he did last year, and sometimes at the end of a race he would find himself gasping for air. His girlfriend was complaining that she didn't like kissing him—she thought his breath smelled like stale smoke. And he was getting tired of hiding his smoking from his parents.

But it wasn't as easy to stop as Tim had thought it would be. He kept getting headaches, and he felt dizzy and tired. He couldn't concentrate at school. All he could think about was smoking. He was only 18 years old. He couldn't be addicted to cigarettes—could he?

What Tim may not know about smoking is that dealing with a disappointed girlfriend and disapproving coach are just the beginning of his problems. His poor performance on the track is a symptom of some of the health effects of smoking—a reduced oxygen carrying capacity of the blood, and an increased resting heart rate and basil metabolic rate. The fact that Tim is having trouble quitting shows just how addictive cigarettes can be.

the soft tissue of your mouth. And teens who try smokeless tobacco are more likely to eventually smoke cigarettes than teens who do not use smokeless tobacco.

SECONDHAND SMOKE

In recent years, we have learned that smoking does not simply pose a health risk to the smoker, but also to anyone around him or her. Initial studies and research into the dangers of tobacco use had focused on the person using the tobacco products, but by 1985 the U.S. Surgeon General had published a report outlining concerns about exposure to secondhand smoke in the workplace. In 1986, the published *Surgeon General's Report* contained research detailing that secondhand smoke could lead to lung cancer.

What is secondhand smoke? When tobacco is smoked—whether in a cigarette, cigar, or pipe—the smoke that is produced can be described in two forms. Mainstream smoke is the smoke that is then drawn through the mouthpiece of the cigar, cigarette, or pipe. Sidestream smoke is the smoke that is produced by the burning tobacco—the smoke that escapes between the smoker's inhaling and exhaling. The chemical compositions of these two types of smoke are different. Studies have shown that the sidestream smoke in general has higher concentrations of toxic substances, including tar, nicotine, and carbon monoxide.

The mixture of mainstream smoke (exhaled by a smoker) and sidestream smoke goes out into the air whenever someone is smoking and where anyone nearby can inhale it. When someone breathes in this tobacco smoke, that person is described as a passive smoker. Such people are subjected to many of the same hazards of smoking simply by being in a place where they are inhaling the tobacco smoke.

Secondhand smoke, or environmental tobacco smoke (ETS) as it is also called, has been proven to contribute to the development of certain types of cancer—particularly lung

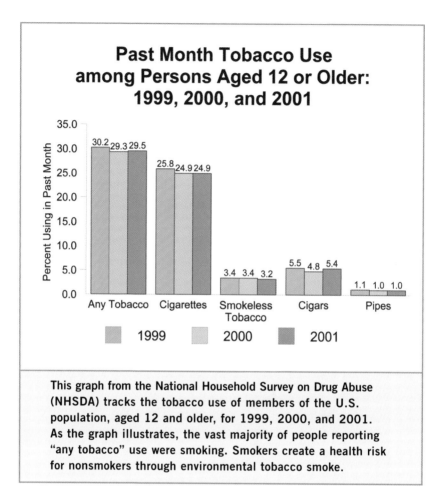

Past Month Tobacco Use among Persons Aged 12 or Older: 1999, 2000, and 2001

This graph from the National Household Survey on Drug Abuse (NHSDA) tracks the tobacco use of members of the U.S. population, aged 12 and older, for 1999, 2000, and 2001. As the graph illustrates, the vast majority of people reporting "any tobacco" use were smoking. Smokers create a health risk for nonsmokers through environmental tobacco smoke.

cancer—in nonsmokers. In 1991, the National Institute for Occupational Safety and Health officially recognized ETS as a potential occupational hazard because of its links to cancer and recommended that employees' exposure to ETS be reduced to the lowest possible levels. Many office buildings and public places now severely limit where smoking can take place to prevent other people from being inadvertently exposed to ETS. In some businesses, smoking is banned altogether, and smokers must leave the building or structure before lighting up.

California has led the United States in its effort to eliminate exposure to ETS by banning indoor smoking in many public places or, in some cases, by limiting it to separately ventilated areas. In California, all indoor workplaces are smoke-free—including bars and restaurants.

ETS has been categorized by the National Institutes of Health as a "known" human carcinogen. This means that clear links have been established between exposure to ETS and the development of cancer in humans. In addition to links to lung cancer, ETS has also been associated with an increased risk of heart disease in nonsmokers.

Statistics underline this risk. The Centers for Disease Control and Prevention reports that ETS causes approximately 3,000 lung cancer deaths annually among adult nonsmokers, as well as an estimated 62,000 deaths from coronary heart disease. In children, ETS contributes to their having more frequent and more severe asthma attacks, as well as lower-respiratory tract

SMOKING: The Rest of the Story

In a study of 557 high school students 13 to 19 years old, researchers found several important differences between smokers and nonsmokers:

- Smokers were two times more likely to have suffered from daily coughing spells for more than three months.

- Smokers were three times more likely to have increased amounts of phlegm every day.

- Smokers were two times more likely to feel shortness of breath when hurrying.

- Smokers were more likely to have experience wheezing or asthma and to have had a chest cold that lasted for a week than nonsmokers.

infections. Research has also linked ETS exposure to an increased risk for Sudden Infant Death Syndrome (SIDS) and ear infections.

A FINAL WORD OF CAUTION

Besides the direct consequences of smoking, there are other indirect consequences of smoking that should make any teen who is thinking about smoking think again. Research has shown that smoking is a risk factor for other drug use. This means that cigarette smoking is often a first step to other illegal behavior—drinking alcohol and using other illegal drugs. Many studies have demonstrated that people who use illegal drugs such as marijuana or cocaine began by using cigarettes, alcohol, or both. Although not every cigarette smoker goes on to abuse other drugs, there is strong evidence that smoking cigarettes, particularly if you begin before the age of 17, can lead to the abuse of other drugs.

4

Teenage Trends and Attitudes

Every day, approximately 4,800 young people between the ages of 11 and 17 will smoke their first cigarette. Of these, almost half will become regular smokers. These teens don't start out smoking with the hope that they will become addicted to nicotine. They smoke because they think it will make them more popular or somehow help them to fit in with their friends and peers. They begin smoking because they believe that smoking will somehow make them feel better about themselves. For some, smoking can be a gesture of independence, a way to signal that no adult can make your decisions for you. It may be a way to "break the rules."

Teens may choose to smoke in response to advertisements. Even though it is illegal to target underage smokers in advertising campaigns, promotional marketing of cigarettes is intended to depict a happier, more glamorous lifestyle for those who smoke. Movies that show popular actors and actresses smoking contribute to this image-building and convey the idea that smoking is sophisticated.

Finally, some teens begin smoking in response to the influence of a family member. If you grow up in a household in which one or both parents smoke, their patterns and behavior may determine the choices you make about cigarettes and other nicotine products. Smoking can become part of meals—a final course at the end—and a part of the family's daily routine.

Other factors may mark a teen's likelihood to begin smoking.

Smoking really is a dirty habit when you look at it up close, and no one plans to become addicted or put themselves at risk for disease when they start. There are many factors that motivate someone to smoke their first cigarette, such as a friend or family member's influence, advertisements, or a desire to rebel.

Teens with poor grades and low self-esteem are more likely to smoke than their peers. Teens from single-parent families are more likely to smoke than their peers. Teens from low-income households are also more likely to become smokers. Teens who have suffered abuse, who have grown up in a violent household,

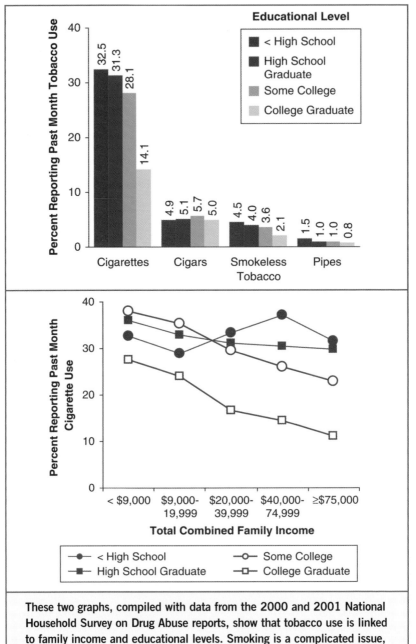

These two graphs, compiled with data from the 2000 and 2001 National Household Survey on Drug Abuse reports, show that tobacco use is linked to family income and educational levels. Smoking is a complicated issue, with many factors influencing a teen's decision to smoke.

or who are in a household in which a family member suffered from mental illness or substance abuse problems or had been jailed are more likely to smoke.

Few teens who do begin smoking are unaware of the risks. But, they view the hazards of smoking as something that happens when they are older, say in 40 or 50 years. They believe that they will easily be able to stop before they reach the age when smoking will seriously damage their health. But they are wrong.

MYTHS ABOUT SMOKING

How smart are you about tobacco? There are a number of myths about tobacco products. The following section, based on facts collected by the Centers for Disease Control and Prevention (CDC), will help you compare some of the myths about nicotine and smoking with reality.

Myth: It's easy to quit smoking because nicotine isn't that addictive.

Fact: About two-thirds of all young smokers say they want to stop. Seven out of 10 say that they wish they had never started smoking. According to the CDC, when teen smokers are asked about whether they will continue to smoke, only 5 percent say they think they will still be smoking in five years, but about 75 percent are still smoking seven years later.

Myth: Smoking is only harmful if you smoke for a long time—20 years or more.

Fact: Once you begin smoking, you begin damaging your body almost immediately. Teen smokers cough and wheeze more. They produce more phlegm, their lungs are smaller, and their hearts are weaker.

Myth: Smoking is a cheap habit.

Fact: Smoking a pack a day (20 cigarettes a day) costs a smoker $1000-$1500 dollars per year, depending on which state you live in.

Myth: Chewing tobacco is safer and less addictive than cigarettes.

Fact: All products that contain nicotine, including chewing tobacco and snuff, are dangerous and addictive. One "dip" of smokeless tobacco can contain as much nicotine as several cigarettes. Chewing tobacco causes cracked lips, mouth sores that don't heal, and bleeding gums. It stains your teeth yellowish-brown and causes bad breath. It can cause several types of cancer, including cancer of the mouth, and can contribute to heart disease and stroke.

Myth: Since the tobacco in cigarettes comes from a plant, it's natural and not that bad.

Fact: Cigarette smoke contains ammonia (used to clean toilets), cyanide (used to kill rats), and formaldehyde (used to preserve dead bodies for dissection). More than 40 of the chemicals contained in cigarette smoke are known to cause cancer in people or animals. And chewing tobacco is no better—it contains high concentrations of nitrosamines, which are chemicals known to cause cancer.

Myth: Compared to all the other dangers in the world, smoking is relatively harmless.

Fact: One out of every five deaths in the United States is caused by a smoking-related illness—more than 400,000 people per year. That's more than AIDS, alcohol, drug abuse, car crashes, murders, fires, and suicides combined.

Marla wanted her mother to stop smoking. She hated listening to her mother's horrible, hacking cough every morning, hated watching her panic if she had forgotten to buy more cigarettes at the store. She worried about her mother's health, worried that she might not be there for the important moments in Marla's life. She had watched her grandmother die a slow and painful death from lung cancer. She didn't want to see the same thing happen to her mother. Marla had talked to her mother about quitting. And her mother had even promised to try. But soon she would run into some sort of stress and reach again for the cigarettes. She would promise to try again— once the "busy time" at work had ended, once the holidays were over, once she reached a particular age. But she could never seem to find the right time.

What Marla may not know is that her mother can't seem to find the right time because she is addicted to nicotine. Most smokers know that smoking is a harmful habit, and most plan to quit. According to a poll conducted by the CDC, 95% of teens who reported smoking in high school did not think they would be smoking five years later, but more that 75% of them were still smoking seven years later.

AN EXPENSIVE HABIT

Nicotine is a highly addictive drug. At the beginning, when you first start smoking, your body gives you clues that you are doing something dangerous. You may cough and choke or feel nauseous. But if you continue smoking, these warning signs disappear. Your body grows accustomed to the doses of nicotine, and it knows to crave them when they are gone.

So if the numbers are correct—if approximately one out

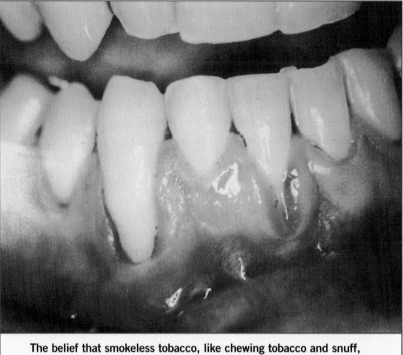

The belief that smokeless tobacco, like chewing tobacco and snuff, is safer than cigarettes is a myth. The gum damage suffered by this patient was caused by smokeless tobacco.

of every five teenagers in the United States smokes—than what's the harm? Nicotine is not an illegal substance. If you are 18 years old or older, you can buy tobacco products everywhere. If nicotine is so dangerous, why aren't cigarettes and other tobacco products illegal?

The answer is that it is illegal to sell tobacco products to anyone who is younger than 18 years old. A store that sells cigarettes or other tobacco products is required to ask for identification from anyone who looks younger than 27 years old to confirm that they are old enough to legally purchase these items.

There are certain groups who are lobbying to make all tobacco products illegal. They feel that the diseases caused by tobacco products have contributed to escalating medical costs. The *Journal of the American Medical Association* has reported that tobacco use is the cause of about one in every five deaths in the United States, labeling it "the main cause of preventable death and disease in the country." As discussed earlier, some states have taken legal action against tobacco manufacturers so that they can recover the costs spent in providing medical care for smokers.

In addition to taking legal action against tobacco companies, some states have levied heavier taxes on cigarettes, hoping that higher prices will encourage people to smoke less, or quit altogether. In a World Bank study, it was shown that for every 10 percent increase in the price of cigarettes, approximately four percent of smokers quit.

In fact, the United States has, on average, higher prices for a pack of cigarettes than many other countries in the world. It may surprise you to learn that the United Kingdom is one of the few countries whose price per pack of cigarettes is higher than that of the United States. Compare these 2001 prices (in American dollars) for a pack of cigarettes around the world:

- $0.85 in Brazil
- $0.98 in Russia
- $1.24 in India
- $1.30 in Saudi Arabia
- $1.55 in Kenya
- $1.90 in Ecuador
- $2.34 in Japan
- $2.81 in Germany
- $3.40 in Canada
- $3.71 in the United States
- $6.24 in the United Kingdom

THE UGLY TRUTH ABOUT NICOTINE

Tobacco use can quickly become an expensive habit. Apart from the costs of the tobacco products themselves—the cigarettes or cigars, the lighters or matches—there are a number of hidden costs to using products containing nicotine.

Tobacco use affects your health. If you smoke regularly, or frequently use any tobacco products, you are much more susceptible to a number of illnesses and diseases. You will need more medical care, and visits to the doctor's office or the pharmacy will become more and more frequent the longer you smoke.

You may believe that you can quit whenever you want to, but it doesn't take a lifetime of smoking to make someone an addict. A study of teens who smoked 100 cigarettes or more in their lifetime shows that most would like to quit but are unable to do so. And nearly all heavy smokers report that they first began smoking before they finished high school. Remember that the younger you are when you begin, the more likely you are to become severely addicted to nicotine and the harder it will be for you to quit.

There are a number of reasons why you should not begin smoking and why you should consider quitting if you have already started to smoke:

- **Your health.** Smoking is the leading cause of lung cancer as well as cancer of the mouth, bladder, throat, kidney, and pancreas. Smokeless tobacco is no better— it causes mouth cancer, tooth loss, and many other illnesses. Teens who smoke report hacking coughs, increase phlegm, respiratory illnesses, and difficulty maintaining the same level of physical activity and endurance.

- **Your body's development.** Teenage smokers risk affecting their body's growth and maturation at

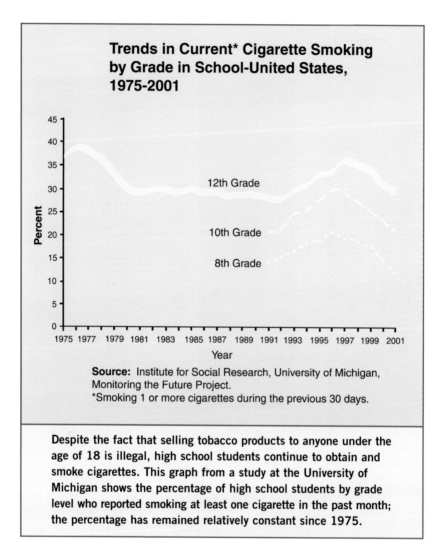

Trends in Current* Cigarette Smoking by Grade in School-United States, 1975-2001

Percent

12th Grade

10th Grade

8th Grade

Year

Source: Institute for Social Research, University of Michigan, Monitoring the Future Project.
*Smoking 1 or more cigarettes during the previous 30 days.

Despite the fact that selling tobacco products to anyone under the age of 18 is illegal, high school students continue to obtain and smoke cigarettes. This graph from a study at the University of Michigan shows the percentage of high school students by grade level who reported smoking at least one cigarette in the past month; the percentage has remained relatively constant since 1975.

the very time when the body is still changing and developing. Smoking affects the development of the lungs and can lead to such potentially fatal illnesses as chronic bronchitis, stroke, and heart disease.

• **Becoming addicted.** The younger you are when you begin to smoke, the more likely you are to become

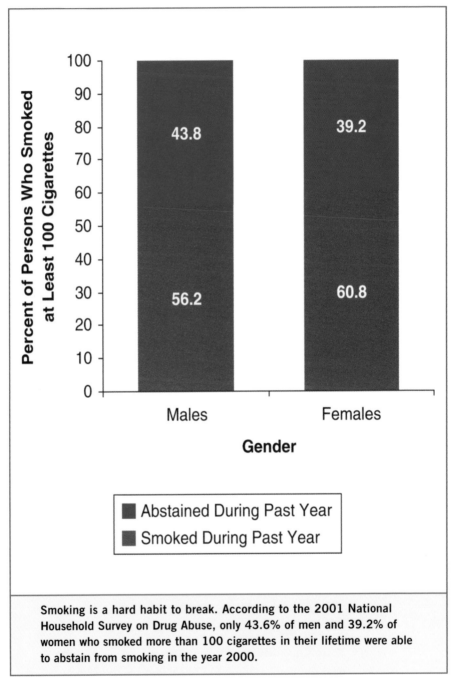

Smoking is a hard habit to break. According to the 2001 National Household Survey on Drug Abuse, only 43.6% of men and 39.2% of women who smoked more than 100 cigarettes in their lifetime were able to abstain from smoking in the year 2000.

addicted to nicotine. Remember, nearly half a
million Americans die from tobacco-related
illnesses each year—and almost all of them began
smoking before they were 18.

- **The cost.** Smoking is an expensive habit. Just think:
  a $3.25 pack-per-day habit adds up to more than
  $1,100 a year. Imagine what you could buy with
  an extra $1,100 a year if you weren't spending it
  on cigarettes.

- **The look.** You may believe that smoking makes you
  look more glamorous, but fast forward a few years
  to the point at which regular smoking has really
  changed the way you look. Smoking stains your
  teeth. It can stain your fingertips. It causes premature wrinkling in your face, particularly around
  your mouth. It causes bad breath. Your hair and
  clothes smell of stale tobacco smoke. Chewing
  tobacco causes cracked lips, sores, white spots,
  and even bleeding in your mouth.

- **The people around you.** Smoking doesn't only
  affect your health; it affects the health of anyone
  who is around you when you are smoking. Approximately 3,000 nonsmokers die of lung cancer each
  year—just from breathing other people's smoke.

THE LAST WORD

At times it seems as if everyone is smoking, and it is hard to be
the one who says no when your friends are lighting up. But
there are other teens who are choosing not to smoke, and
the number is on the rise. A 2001 study by the CDC found
that smoking among U.S. high school students is on the
decline. Only 28.5% of high school students reported smoking,
marking a decline from the 36.4% who said that they smoked

SMOKING IN THE MOVIES
Does it influence teen smokers?

Julia Roberts chain-smoked throughout *My Best Friend's Wedding* in 1997. Leonardo DiCaprio polluted the skies over Thailand in 2000 with cigarette after cigarette in *The Beach*. Even the adorable little green aliens from *Men in Black II* puffed on cigarettes in 2002. Experts fear that Hollywood blockbuster movies are sending the wrong message to teens by showing some of the most famous actors and actresses lighting up cigarettes. The writers, directors, and studios that produce these movies claim they are merely imitating real-life trends and attitudes toward smoking.

What's the truth? Let's take a look at the some of the straight facts on smoking and the movies. According to studies conducted by Stanton Glantz, a professor of medicine at the University of California, San Francisco:

- The use of cigarettes on screen did not decline over the decades, even though the number of American smokers dwindled from 42.4% in 1964 to 25.5% in 1994.

- The number of young adults smoking on camera more than doubled from 21% in the 1960s to 45% in the 1980s, compared to only 26% in real life.

- Although only 19% of Americans of high socioeconomic status smoke, 57% of those playing roles of characters with high socioeconomic status smoke.

- The heroes in movies, as contrasted with those who played villains or bit parts, smoked three times as often as their counterparts in real life (by age, race, and gender).

As these facts suggest, movies may not, in fact, reflect real-life trends and attitudes towards smoking in the United

States. But as researchers have discovered, on-screen smoking does have a significant impact on teens and their willingness to smoke. Professor James Sargent and his colleagues at Dartmouth Medical School surveyed 4,919 American children aged 9-15 years about the amount of smoking they had seen at the movies and whether they had ever tried smoking. In a study published in the December 15, 2001 issue of the *British Medical Journal*, the Dartmouth researchers reported that the more teens are exposed to smoking in the movies, the more likely they are to experiment with smoking themselves:

- 4.9% of teens who viewed 0-50 occurrences of smoking in movies tried smoking themselves.

- 13.7% of teens who saw 51-100 occurrences of smoking in movies tried smoking themselves.

- 22.1% of teens who saw 101-150 occurrences of smoking in movies tried smoking themselves.

- 31.3% of teens who saw more than 150 occurrences of smoking in movies tried smoking themselves.

The researchers involved in the Dartmouth study concluded that there is a direct association between seeing tobacco use in movies and trying cigarettes, a finding that supports the hypothesis that smoking in movies influences teen trends and attitudes toward smoking.

Sources:
Smoke Free Movies, http://smokefreemovies.ucsf.edu
Action on Smoking and Health, http://ash.org
Sargent, James D. et al. "Effect of seeing tobacco use in films on trying smoking among adolescents: cross sectional study." BMJ 323 (2001):1394.

in 1996. And only 13.8% described themselves as "frequent" smokers. The declining rate is thought to be due to new awareness of the dangers of smoking, as well as to the increasing cost of cigarettes.

So who actually is smoking? The recent research shows that boys are slightly more likely to smoke than girls and that white students are more likely to describe themselves as smokers than African-American or Hispanic students.

The health risks are clear. Few teens claim that they are unaware of the hazards of smoking. But still many start smoking and then find it difficult to give up nicotine.

Perhaps you have tried smoking and are finding it difficult to quit. Maybe you have a friend or family member whose

TEENS WHO SMOKE

You may think you know everything there is to know about teens who smoke. But take a look at these statistics from the Centers for Disease Control and Prevention:

- Early signs of heart disease and stroke can be found in teens who smoke.

- People who smoke live on average seven years less than those who never smoked.

- The resting heart rates of young smokers are two to three beats faster than those of nonsmokers.

- Teenage smokers are more likely to see doctors or other health care workers for emotional or psychological problems.

- Teens who smoke are three times more likely than non-smokers to use alcohol, eight times more likely to use marijuana, and 22 times more likely to use cocaine.

tobacco habit worries you, and you would like to encourage the person to stop. In the next chapter, we will examine the ways in which nicotine addiction can be treated and the resources that are available for help.

5

Nicotine Addiction

Nicotine is a very addictive drug. Taken in large enough amounts, nicotine can kill you. But the amount of nicotine in the average cigarette is very small—only about 8 or 9 milligrams (to understand exactly how small an amount this is, remember that it takes more than 28,000 milligrams to equal 1 ounce).

There may be 8 or 9 milligrams of nicotine in the average cigarette, but a smoker inhales even less. The amount of nicotine a smoker actually inhales from the average cigarette is between 1 and 1.5 milligrams. But even in this tiny amount, nicotine goes to work on your body, changing the way your brain and organs function. This is precisely why nicotine is so dangerous. Even in such small amounts, it proves addictive and alters your body's functioning.

Nicotine is addictive both physically (your body becomes accustomed to a certain amount of nicotine in your system and suffers when that nicotine is withdrawn) and psychologically. Both addictions are difficult to break. Your body feels stressed and anxious when you stop smoking. But there are also things in your environment that remind you of smoking and make you think again and again about smoking. Perhaps you always smoke after school, or after a certain class period, or with a particular group of friends. Maybe you are surrounded by people who smoke (friends, a parent), and seeing them smoke makes you crave a cigarette even more.

Simple acts or places may provide these visual clues—triggers—that remind you of smoking. Certain situations can also be

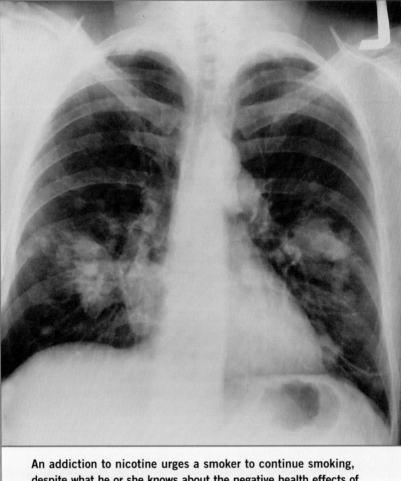

An addiction to nicotine urges a smoker to continue smoking, despite what he or she knows about the negative health effects of smoking. This diagnostic chest X-ray of a smoker's lungs reveals a dark spot at the bottom of the left lung, which could possibly be a cancerous growth. Fortunately, even heavy smokers can reap the benefits of quitting: a study reported in the *British Medical Journal* in 2000 found that smokers who abstained from smoking for less than 10 years lowered their risk of developing lung cancer by 33%.

triggers—a stressful relationship, a difficult test, or pressure from parents or teachers. All these can contribute to your need for nicotine.

It is important to remember that whether you are trying to quit the habit or you are trying to help a friend quit, an addiction to nicotine has developed over time, and it will take time and effort to stop.

REASONS FOR QUITTING

Take a good look at the ways in which nicotine affects your body (Chapter 3). Nicotine is hazardous—even to people who haven't been smoking for a very long time, and particularly to young smokers. Your health should be your number one reason for giving up nicotine.

One out of every three smokers will die earlier than they should have—because of smoking. Smoking can cause cancer, heart disease, emphysema, and stroke. It can reduce your physical fitness and, if you are an athlete, hamper your endurance and performance. Young teens who smoke cough more, have more phlegm, and are more prone to respiratory infections. As soon as you stop smoking, your body will get to work repairing the damage smoking has done. You will quickly breathe better and feel better.

Giving up nicotine will improve not only your health, but also the health of the people around you. Secondhand smoke, or environmental tobacco smoke, has been proved to affect the health of nonsmokers. Breathing in your cigarette or cigar smoke can place the people around you at increased risk for developing breathing problems, cancer, and heart disease.

There are other reasons to stop smoking. Purchasing nicotine products is not just hazardous for teens—it is illegal for anyone under the age of 18.

Think also about the financial incentives—the money you spend on cigarettes and the money you will spend in the future if you continue to smoke. Imagine how you could spend that money if it weren't used for cigarettes.

HELPING SOMEONE YOU LOVE

Perhaps it is not your own smoking that has prompted you to pick up this book, but the nicotine use of someone you care about—a friend or family member. How can you help someone else give up smoking?

Smoking is a personal choice, and it is up to the smoker to decide to stop. But there are some ways that you can encourage someone to examine his or her habit and think about its consequences.

Remind them of the dangers smoking creates for their health, not in an accusing way, but in a way that lets them know that you care about them. Perhaps you have heard them coughing frequently or struggling for breath, or seen that they are no longer able to run or walk as fast as they used to. Let them know that these things concern you and that you are worried

RESOURCES THAT CAN HELP

Your health care provider, school counselor, or phone book can provide you with a list of local organizations and programs designed to help people stop smoking or give up tobacco products. There are also a number of national organizations that can provide helpful resources or information on quitting smoking.

You may want to begin by checking these web sites:

- Agency for Health Care Policy and Research: *www.ahcpr.gov*

- American Cancer Society: *www.cancer.org*

- American Heart Association: *www.americanheart.org*

- American Lung Association: *www.lungusa.org*

- National Cancer Institute: *www.cancer.gov*

- Office on Smoking and Health (CDC): *www.cdc.gov/tobacco*

about the impact that their nicotine use is having on their health, both now and in the future.

Be specific, but not confrontational, about how their smoking is causing you concern. Make sure to offer your support if they choose to quit. Offer your help in finding the right program to help them stop smoking. Understand that they may need to drastically change their routines to avoid situations that make them want to reach for a cigarette. Remember that a habit like smoking, particularly if it has been habit for many years, may take time to break and may require more than one attempt to stop.

FIRST STEPS TOWARD SUCCESS

Most successful programs designed to help people give up their dependence on nicotine are based on certain key steps, including:

- Preparation
- Support
- Learning new behaviors and routines
- Medication
- Understanding that relapses can happen

Let's take a look at each of these steps to better understand the process of stopping an addiction.

Preparing to Stop Smoking

The first stage is preparation. This involves more than simply deciding to stop smoking, although this, of course, is a critical step. You need to carefully examine your own habit as a key to breaking the cycle.

Think about the times when you smoke. Are you most likely to smoke in the mornings, afternoons, or evenings? During the week or weekends? Are there certain triggers to your smoking? Are you in a particular place? With a certain group of people? By yourself? What emotions are you most

Understanding the patterns and behaviors associated with smoking are essential to breaking the cycle. Any smoker who wishes to quit must know the "who, what, when, where, and why" of his or her smoking habit in order to avoid the triggers that may lead to a relapse.

often experiencing before you start smoking, and what situations prompt you to reach for a cigarette? Is it because you want to "fit in" with a particular group of people? Is it when you are anxious? Or depressed? Or lonely?

You may find it helpful to keep a record of the "who, what, when, where, and why" of your personal smoking habit. This information will help you to prepare in advance for situations that may make your efforts to quit more difficult and will help you to avoid triggers that may throw obstacles in your path.

Part of the preparation process is picking an official

date—a date when you will stop smoking. Avoid days that might be particularly stressful, like a holiday or the beginning of a new school year. If you are more likely to smoke during the school week, you may want to pick a Saturday for your quit date to help make it easier to get started.

Clean up your environment before your quit day. Throw out all the cigarettes, ashtrays, matches, and lighters. Don't leave anything around that might tempt you to smoke "just one last cigarette."

Make a list of all of the reasons you want to quit and place it somewhere where you will be able to easily see the reasons why you need to stop. This will help encourage you if you begin to question why you are quitting.

Finally, be prepared for what will happen. Remember that your body has grown accustomed to having a certain amount of nicotine, and that it will crave it when it is gone. Your body will experience certain physical symptoms as it begins to recover from the nicotine. Some ex-smokers feel sleepy or lightheaded. Some feel very excited or nervous. Some feel irritable or experience headaches. Others crave sweets.

Plan to get some kind of exercise, particularly in the beginning. Walking, biking, swimming, or any other form of physical exercise will do more than simply distract you— exercise is a proven way to reduce stress. If smoking has been your way of coping with stress, exercise is a great replacement. It will make you feel better—and healthier.

Getting Support

A second key component in breaking an addiction is having a source of support, to encourage you in your efforts and keep you focused on your goals. Share your plan with an understanding friend or family member. Let him or her know what you are trying to accomplish and ask for help. Perhaps you have a friend who will be willing to have you phone to report on your progress or to ask for encouragement if you are craving a cigarette. Maybe a family member would be willing to help you break your routine by going somewhere new or trying a new activity.

If you have a health care provider, school counselor, or teacher or pastor whom you trust, he or she might also be helpful sources of support and encouragement. This support person may be able to provide you with information on organizations and support groups in your area.

If you have friends or family members who smoke, let them know that you are going to quit. Ask them not to smoke in front of you or to leave their cigarettes in places where you are going to be.

Many ex-smokers also benefit from the support and encouragement of trained professionals and others who have stopped smoking. Local hospitals and health care centers frequently sponsor programs designed to help people give up tobacco. Check the listings in your phone book, or call your area's health department to find out what programs are available. A list of additional sources of support for those trying to quit can be found at the end of this book.

New Behaviors, New Routines

A key to successfully breaking any damaging or dangerous habit is understanding what led to it in the first place. As part of the preparation stage, you examined many of the factors that contribute to your urge to smoke. Now, with that information, you will want to eliminate those triggers as much as possible or to determine new ways to cope with those situations—ways that don't involve nicotine.

If you most often want to smoke when you are by yourself or feeling lonely, do your best to avoid those situations. Volunteer at a hospital or shelter. Sign up for an after-school activity. Participate in a club or sport. Look for a part-time job. Do something to keep yourself busy. Go for a walk or a run. Plan out each day in advance so that you will be busy, and avoid too much "alone time." Include something in each day that you will enjoy—a treat for each smoke-free day.

Change your routine. Get up early enough to have breakfast before school. Avoid the places where your friends may hang out to smoke. Take a careful look at what you are eating to make sure that your diet is balanced and healthy, with plenty of protein and carbohydrates. Drink more water. Get plenty of

Alisha first tried smoking when she was by herself and bored. She took a cigarette that she found from a pack that her aunt had left on the kitchen counter. Nobody else was in the house, so she went into her room, opened a window, and smoked. That first cigarette wasn't so great, and neither was the second one that she tried a few days later. But Alisha liked the idea of smoking, even if the reality of it wasn't so great, and so she kept trying. Now she looked forward to coming home from school to an empty house, slipping up to her room, lighting a cigarette, and then watching the smoke curl up and out the open window. It makes her feel calm and gives her a feeling of power—of having some secret part of herself that no one else can share.

Alisha has tried to quit, but she always seems to grab a cigarette as soon as she walks in the door after school. She does it without thinking, almost like she's on automatic pilot. It is just something that has become a part of her afternoons, filling the time before her parents come home from work.

What Alisha may not know is that if she is serious about quitting, she needs to examine the behaviors and routines associated with her smoking habit. A smoker is more likely to quit if he or she can avoid the patterns, places, and times that may lead to a relapse, and replace these triggers with new hobbies and activities.

sleep. Do everything possible to keep your body feeling healthy and strong.

Find new ways to cope with stress and to relax. Exercise can help. So can taking a hot bath, talking with a friend, or reading a good book. You may find it helpful to keep a journal, where you can record your feelings and your progress.

Medication

Certain medications have also proved to be helpful to those trying to give up tobacco products. *It is important to remember that anyone under the age of 18 should consult a health care provider—a doctor or nurse—before taking any of these medications.* A health care provider is able to give you advice about what type of medication, if any, is appropriate for you and about treatments that might be hazardous to your health.

The FDA has approved five medications for people trying to quit smoking. Again, remember that these are approved for adult use. Teens should not use these without first consulting their health care provider.

- Nicotine gum—available over-the-counter. It releases small amounts of nicotine into the body, cutting down on some of the physical symptoms of withdrawal. The recommended treatment period for people using nicotine chewing gum is 12 weeks. Generally, adults chew 10 to 15 pieces of gum per day. Drinks containing caffeine, such as soda and coffee, should not be used before, during, or after chewing the gum.

- Nicotine patch—available by prescription and over-the-counter. The nicotine patch works by providing a small dose of nicotine throughout the day, helping to relieve the physical craving for nicotine. A new patch must be applied to the upper body each day. Some patches must be removed at night; others are worn for 24 hours. Patches are available in either 6-week or 12-week treatments.

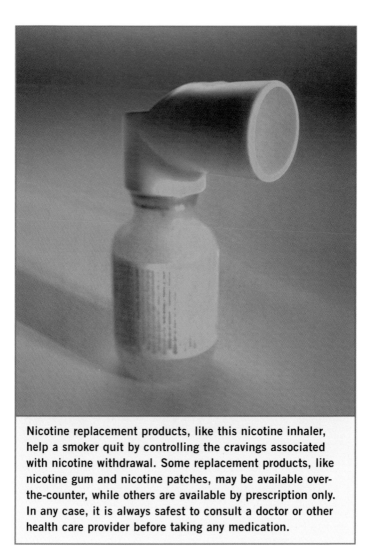

Nicotine replacement products, like this nicotine inhaler, help a smoker quit by controlling the cravings associated with nicotine withdrawal. Some replacement products, like nicotine gum and nicotine patches, may be available over-the-counter, while others are available by prescription only. In any case, it is always safest to consult a doctor or other health care provider before taking any medication.

- Nicotine inhaler—available by prescription only.

- Nicotine nasal spray—available by prescription only.

- Non-nicotine pill—available by prescription only. This pill, Bupropion SR, also known as Bupropion hydrochloride or Zyban, was approved by the FDA in 1997 for use in combating nicotine addiction

Nicotine replacement products have proved successful in helping many smokers stop smoking. They provide less nicotine than a smoker would get from cigarettes, but help ease or relieve some of the physical symptoms of withdrawal. It is critical that smokers stop completely before using any nicotine replacement product.

Mistakes Can Happen—and Relapses, Too

It can take more than one attempt to quit. Many people need two or three tries before being able to successfully stop smoking. And most relapses occur within the first three months after quitting. Don't be discouraged if you don't succeed the first time. It can take practice to overcome your physical addiction to nicotine and break the habit of smoking. But more than 45 million Americans have done it.

6

Exploring Additional Resources

We have discussed how nicotine can affect your body. We have learned a bit about the history of tobacco use, particularly in the United States. We have examined some of the legal issues surrounding tobacco products and how those laws have changed. We have read about teens making decisions about tobacco products and learned more about who is likely to smoke or use tobacco and why. We have taken a look at some of the myths surrounding nicotine and discovered how, just like any drug, it can become addictive. We have discussed how nicotine acts in your body and why it is such an addictive drug. Most important, we have talked about what to do if you or a friend or family member would like to stop smoking.

If you need assistance, support, or just more information about nicotine, smoking, or tobacco products, you'll find many resources available. Start with the adults you know—a parent, a teacher, your school counselor, a minister, or your doctor or nurse may be able to provide support or suggestions for places where you will find the help you need. There are also a number of organizations that specialize in dealing with smoking-related issues, offering support groups, counseling, an on-line network, or helpful statistics and information.

In addition to the national organizations listed in the following section, your state health department may be able to provide helpful information on local resources, and hospitals and health centers may offer more specialized programs.

BIG TOBACCO TARGETS YOUNG SMOKERS

Lawsuits against big tobacco companies in recent years have made confidential company documents available to the general public. The contents of these documents reveal that tobacco companies have targeted teens and young adults as "replacement customers" for the more than 400,000 smokers who die each year due to smoking-related diseases. Take a look at just a few of the quotes from these documents:

Philip Morris: "Today's teenager is tomorrow's regular customer."

Lorillard Tobacco: "The base of our business is the high school student."

U.S. Tobacco: "Cherry Skoal is for somebody who likes the taste of candy, if you know what I'm saying."

R.J. Reynolds: "If our company is to survive and prosper, over the long term we must get our share of the youth market."

If you decide you don't want to be just another statistic in the big tobacco machine, take advantage of the resources listed in this chapter to quit smoking or become an antismoking activist.

American Cancer Society

A nonprofit organization dedicated to providing research, education, advocacy, and service designed to prevent cancer and save lives. Provides information on the health risks associated with tobacco use.

1599 Clifton Road, NE
Atlanta, GA 30329
1-800-ACS-2345 (1-800-227-2345)
www.cancer.org

American Heart Association

Offers information about tobacco-related heart disease and stroke. Provides educational materials as well as programs at schools, offices, and hospitals designed to help eliminate smoking.

7272 Greenville Avenue

Dallas, TX 75231

1-800-AHA-USA1 (1-800-242-8721)

www.americanheart.org

American Lung Association

Provides materials designed to educate the public about causes of lung disease, including tobacco use. A valuable source of research on the dangers of smoking and on ways to stop.

1740 Broadway, 14th floor

New York, NY 10019

1-800-LUNG-USA (1-800-586-4872)

www.lungusa.org

Campaign for Tobacco-Free Kids

An organization dedicated to protect children and teens from tobacco addiction and exposure to secondhand smoke. Promotes youth advocacy and tobacco control efforts; encourages teens to be activists through its Kick Butts campaign.

1400 Eye Street

Suite 1200

Washington, DC 20005

1-202-296-5469

www.tobaccofreekids.org

Centers for Disease Control and Prevention (CDC)

The U.S. government's center for tobacco and health research. Offers a wide range of information related to smoking and health.

Office on Smoking and Health

Mail Stop K-50

4770 Buford Highway, N.E.

Atlanta, GA 30341-3724

1-770-488-5705

www.cdc.gov

National Cancer Institute

The source of a number of publications on smoking, the NCI has created several programs designed to help people stop smoking and also offers telephone counseling for people trying to quit.

31 Center Drive, MSC-2580

Bethesda, MD 20892

1-800-4-CANCER (1-800-422-6237)

www.cancer.gov

Society for Research on Nicotine and Tobacco (SRNT)

A research organization dedicated to the study of nicotine both from a scientific and social perspective.

7600 Terrace Avenue

Suite 203

Middleton, WI 53562

1-608-836-3787

www.srnt.org

Student Coalition Against Tobacco

A national student organization dedicated to reducing the use of tobacco by teens, campaigning against the tobacco industry's targeting of youth, and reducing exposure to secondhand smoke.

P.O. Box 584

Parkersburg, WV 26102

1-888-234-SCAT (1-888-234-7228)

www.smokefreeair.org

Bibliography

Books and Articles

American Council on Science and Health. *Cigarettes: What the Warning Label Doesn't Tell You.* Amherst, NY: Prometheus Books, 1997.

Brigham, Janet. *Dying to Quit.* Washington, DC: Joseph Henry Press, 1998.

Cordry, Harold V. *Tobacco: A Reference Handbook.* Santa Barbara, CA: ABC-CLIO, Inc., 2001.

Fisher, Edwin B., Jr., and Goldfarb, Toni L. *Seven Steps to a Smoke-free Life.* New York: John Wiley & Sons, Inc., 1998.

Gately, Iain. *Tobacco.* New York: Grove Press, 2001.

Hilts, Philip J. *Smoke Screen.* Reading, MA: Addison-Wesley Publishing Co., Inc., 1996.

Kessler, David. *A Question of Intent.* New York: Public Affairs, 2001.

Krogh, David. *Smoking: The Artificial Passion.* New York: W.H. Freeman and Co., 1991.

Kluger, Richard. *Ashes to Ashes.* New York: Alfred A. Knopf, 1996.

Lynch, Barbara S. and Bonnie, Richard J., eds. *Growing Up Tobacco Free: Preventing Nicotine Addiction in Children and Youths.* Washington, DC: National Academy Press, 1994.

McClam, Erin. "High school teens' smoking declines," *Philadelphia Inquirer,* May 17, 2002, p. A26.

National Cancer Institute. *Changing Adolescent Smoking Prevalence.* Smoking and Tobacco Control Monograph No. 14. Bethesda, MD: U.S. Dept. of Health and Human Services, National Institutes of Health, National Cancer Institute, NIH Pub. No. 02-5806, November 2001.

Parker-Pope, Tara. *Cigarettes: Anatomy of an Industry from Seed to Smoke.* New York: The New Press, 2001.

U.S. Dept. of Health and Human Services. *Preventing Tobacco Use Among Young People: A Report of the Surgeon General.* Atlanta, GA: U.S. Dept. of Health and Human Services, Public Health Service, Centers for Disease Control and Prevention, National Center for Chronic Disease Prevention and Health Promotion, Office on Smoking and Health, 1994.

U.S. Dept. of Health and Human Services. *Smoking Cessation.* Rockville, MD: Public Health Service, Agency for Health Care Policy and Research, 1996.

Walker, Ellen. *Smoker.* San Francisco, CA: Harper & Row, 1990.

Williams, Mary E. and Roleff, Tamara L., eds. *Tobacco and Smoking: Opposing Viewpoints.* San Diego, CA: Greenhaven Press, Inc., 1998.

Websites

www.ahcpr.gov

www.americanheart.org

www.cancer.gov

www.cancer.org

www.cdc.gov/tobacco

www.cnn.com

www.health.org

www.library.ucsf.edu/tobacco

www.lungusa.org

www.medem.com

www.nicotine-anonymous.org

www.nicotinefreekids.com

www.quitnet.org

www.srnt.org

www.surgeongeneral.gov/tobacco

Further Reading

Books

American Council on Science and Health. *Cigarettes: What the Warning Label Doesn't Tell You.* Amherst, NY: Prometheus Books, 1997.

Fisher, Edwin B., Jr., and Goldfarb, Toni L. *Seven Steps to a Smoke-free Life.* New York: John Wiley & Sons, Inc., 1998.

Hilts, Philip J. *Smoke Screen.* Reading, MA: Addison-Wesley Publishing Co., Inc., 1996.

Hyde, Margaret O. *Know About Smoking.* New York: Walker & Co., 1995.

Kluger, Richard. *Ashes to Ashes.* New York: Alfred A. Knopf, 1996.

MacDonald, Joan V. *Tobacco and Nicotine: Drug Dangers.* Berkeley Heights, NJ: Enslow Publishers, 2001.

Websites

The American Cancer Society
www.cancer.org

The American Lung Association
www.lungusa.org

The American Heart Association
www.americanheart.org

The National Cancer Institute
www.cancer.gov

The National Center for Chronic Disease Prevention and Health Promotion Tobacco Information and Prevention Source (TIPS)
www.cdc.gov/tobacco

The National Clearing House for Alcohol and Drug Information
www.health.org

Nicotine Free Kids
www.nicotinefreekids.com

Smoke Free Movies
http://smokefreemovies.ucsf.edu

Index

and tobacco as natural,
64
See also Health effects
of nicotine and
smoking
Teeth, 8, 50, 71
Television, cigarette
advertising banned
from, 33, 35
Terry, Luther, 32
Tobacco industry
and campaign encour-
aging smoking, 31-32
growth of, 25-29
and labels on cigarette
packs, 33
lawsuits against, 38-39,
41-43, 67
and list of additives in
cigarettes, 38

and nicotine level in
cigarettes, 13, 38
and price increase, 38
and response to anti-
smoking campaign,
34-35, 36
and targeting younger
smokers, 33, 36
Tobacco products, 14, 16
availability of, 17
history of, 18, 23-24,
25, 26
smoke from, 11-12, 14
See also Cigarettes
Tobacco sheet, 13
Tolerance, 49, 65
Treatment. *See* Nicotine
addiction, treatment
for
Triggers, 81, 83-84

Trinidad, 21

U.S. Tobacco Company,
31

Vinyl chloride, 13
Virginia, 21-22
Voice, 8, 50
West Indies, 21

Withdrawal, 10, 49, 82
Women
and lung cancer, 30, 36
and smoking cigarettes,
29
World War I, 29
Wrapper leaf, 16

Zyban, 86

Picture Credits

page:

About the Author

Heather Lehr Wagner is a writer and editor. She earned an M.A. from the College of William and Mary and a B.A. from Duke University. She has written several books for teens on global and family issues, and is also the author of *Alcohol* and *Cocaine* in the Drugs: The Straight Facts series. She lives with her husband and their three children in Pennsylvania.

About the Editor

David J. Triggle is a University Professor and a Distinguished Professor in the School of Pharmacy and Pharmaceutical Sciences at the State University of New York at Buffalo. He studied in the United Kingdom and earned his B.Sc. degree in Chemistry from the University of Southampton and a Ph.D. degree in Chemistry at the University of Hull. Following post-doctoral work at the University of Ottawa in Canada and the University of London in the United Kingdom, he assumed a position at the School of Pharmacy at Buffalo. He served as Chairman of the Department of Biochemical Pharmacology from 1971 to 1985 and as Dean of the School of Pharmacy from 1985 to 1995. From 1995 to 2001 he served as the Dean of the Graduate School, and as the University Provost from 2000 to 2001. He is the author of several books dealing with the chemical pharmacology of the autonomic nervous system and drug-receptor interactions, some four hundred scientific publications, and has delivered over one thousand lectures worldwide on his research.

DATE DUE	